MW01222044

10

302.23                    000018154

0  0  0  0  1  8  1  5  4

Web/OV

Web 2.0                    3085

302.23                    000018154

Web/OV

Web 2.0

**DAVIS COLLEGE RESOURCE CENTER**
4747 Monroe Street
Toledo, Ohio  43623
(419) 473-2700

# Web 2.0

# Other Books in the Social Issues Firsthand Series:

# Web 2.0

*Laurie Willis, Book Editor*

**GREENHAVEN PRESS**
*A part of Gale, Cengage Learning*

GALE
CENGAGE Learning

Detroit • New York • San Francisco • New Haven, Conn • Waterville, Maine • London

Christine Nasso, *Publisher*
Elizabeth Des Chenes, *Managing Editor*

© 2009 Greenhaven Press, a part of Gale, Cengage Learning.

Gale and Greenhaven Press are registered trademarks used herein under license.

*For more information, contact:*
Greenhaven Press
27500 Drake Rd.
Farmington Hills, MI 48331-3535
Or you can visit our Internet site at gale.cengage.com

For product information and technology assistance, contact us at

Gale Customer Support, 1-800-877-4253
For permission to use material from this text or product, submit all requests online at
www.cengage.com/permissions

Further permissions questions can be emailed to permissionrequest@cengage.com

Articles in Greenhaven Press anthologies are often edited for length to meet page requirements. In addition, original titles of these works are changed to clearly present the main thesis and to explicitly indicate the author's opinion. Every effort is made to ensure that Greenhaven Press accurately reflects the original intent of the authors. Every effort has been made to trace the owners of copyrighted material.

Cover photograph copyright photos.com/Jupiterimages.

LIBRARY OF CONGRESS CATALOGING-IN-PUBLICATION DATA

Web 2.0 / Laurie Willis, book editor.
     p. cm. -- (Social issues firsthand)
   Includes bibliographical references and index.
   ISBN 978-0-7377-4561-0 (hardcover)
   1. Web 2.0. 2. Social media. 3. World Wide Web--Social aspects. I. Willis, Laurie.
   TK5105.88817.W417 2009
   302.23'1--dc22
                                                         2009016631

Printed in the United States of America
1 2 3 4 5 6 7 13 12 11 10 09

# Contents

## Chapter 1: Online Friends and Community

# Foreword

Social issues are often viewed in abstract terms. Pressing challenges such as poverty, homelessness, and addiction are viewed as problems to be defined and solved. Politicians, social scientists, and other experts engage in debates about the extent of the problems, their causes, and how best to remedy them. Often overlooked in these discussions is the human dimension of the issue. Behind every policy debate over poverty, homelessness, and substance abuse, for example, are real people struggling to make ends meet, to survive life on the streets, and to overcome addiction to drugs and alcohol. Their stories are ubiquitous and compelling. They are the stories of everyday people—perhaps your own family members or friends—and yet they rarely influence the debates taking place in state capitols, the national Congress, or the courts.

The disparity between the public debate and private experience of social issues is well illustrated by looking at the topic of poverty. Each year the U.S. Census Bureau establishes a poverty threshold. A household with an income below the threshold is defined as poor, while a household with an income above the threshold is considered able to live on a basic subsistence level. For example, in 2003 a family of two was considered poor if its income was less than $12,015; a family of four was defined as poor if its income was less than $18,810. Based on this system, the bureau estimates that 35.9 million Americans (12.5 percent of the population) lived below the poverty line in 2003, including 12.9 million children below the age of eighteen.

Commentators disagree about what these statistics mean. Social activists insist that the huge number of officially poor Americans translates into human suffering. Even many families that have incomes above the threshold, they maintain, are likely to be struggling to get by. Other commentators insist that the statistics exaggerate the problem of poverty in the United States. Compared to people in developing countries, they point out, most so-called poor families have a high quality of life. As stated by journalist Fidelis Iyebote, "Cars are owned by 70 percent of 'poor' households. . . . Color televisions belong to 97 percent of the 'poor' [and] videocassette recorders belong to nearly 75 percent. . . . Sixty-four percent have microwave ovens, half own a stereo system, and over a quarter possess an automatic dishwasher."

However, this debate over the poverty threshold and what it means is likely irrelevant to a person living in poverty. Simply put, poor people do not need the government to tell them whether they are poor. They can see it in the stack of bills they cannot pay. They are aware of it when they are forced to choose between paying rent or buying food for their children. They become painfully conscious of it when they lose their homes and are forced to live in their cars or on the streets. Indeed, the written stories of poor people define the meaning of poverty more vividly than a government bureaucracy could ever hope to. Narratives composed by the poor describe losing jobs due to injury or mental illness, depict horrific tales of childhood abuse and spousal violence, recount the loss of friends and family members. They evoke the slipping away of social supports and government assistance, the descent into substance abuse and addiction, the harsh realities of life on the streets. These are the perspectives on poverty that are too often omitted from discussions over the extent of the problem and how to solve it.

Greenhaven Press's *Social Issues Firsthand* series provides a forum for the often-overlooked human perspectives on society's most divisive topics of debate. Each volume focuses on one social issue and presents a collection of ten to sixteen narratives by those who have had personal involvement with the topic. Extra care has been taken to include a diverse range of perspectives. For example, in the volume on adoption, readers will find the stories of birth parents who have made an adoption plan, adoptive parents, and adoptees themselves. After exposure to these varied points of view, the reader will have a clearer understanding that adoption is an intense, emotional experience full of joyous highs and painful lows for all concerned.

The debate surrounding embryonic stem cell research illustrates the moral and ethical pressure that the public brings to bear on the scientific community. However, while nonexperts often criticize scientists for not considering the potential negative impact of their work, ironically the public's reaction against such discoveries can produce harmful results as well. For example, although the outcry against embryonic stem cell research in the United States has resulted in fewer embryos being destroyed, those with Parkinson's, such as actor Michael J. Fox, have argued that prohibiting the development of new stem cell lines ultimately will prevent a timely cure for the disease that is killing Fox and thousands of others.

Each book in the series contains several features that enhance its usefulness, including an in-depth introduction, an annotated table of contents, bibliographies for further research, a list of organizations to contact, and a thorough index. These elements—combined with the poignant voices of people touched by tragedy and triumph—make the Social Issues Firsthand series a valuable resource for research on today's topics of political discussion.

# Introduction

The term "Web 2.0" came into common usage after O'Reilly Media hosted a conference in 2004 called Web 2.0. It seems appropriate that Web 2.0 is named in a similar manner that many software companies use to describe updates, but the term refers more to a change in how the Internet is used, more than any one particular change in the software itself. There is no clearly agreed-upon definition of what Web 2.0 is, but it can be described fairly well by comparing it to the old Web—now referred to as "Web 1.0."

In a Web 1.0 world, Web sites were usually developed by an individual or organization to impart content to the rest of the world. Users had to go to the Web site to see the information that was provided. The site content was relatively static, and only a Webmaster held the magic key to gain access and update the site.

Web 2.0 marks a major shift in the way the Internet is used. A user no longer has to visit a site to see recent site updates. The user can subscribe to an RSS feed, which sends the updated content to a place of the user's choosing, usually an RSS reader, sometimes called an aggregator. The user can receive updates on any site of interest, and read them all in one place.

Content is no longer controlled solely by a Webmaster. Instead, it is a collaborative effort between a whole community of people. Many Web 2.0 sites provide very little native content. They merely provide a platform for users to upload content of their own. YouTube (videos) and Flickr (photos) are examples of this type of site.

Online journals called "blogs" are another example, and there are many popular sites that host blogs and provide templates to make blog setup and use simple enough that anyone can have a blog. "Microblogging" is also becoming popular, with Twitter being the first site to support and encourage multitudes of microbloggers. The premise of Twitter is to answer the question, "What are you doing right now?" in 140 characters or less, and to share those answers with the world.

Another key Web 2.0 feature is its interactive nature. People may use a "comments" feature to respond to someone else's blog, photos, or video posting. An online conversation may ensue, and may include others who are interested in the topic. Some Web 2.0 applications are produced collaboratively. Wikipedia, for example, is an online encyclopedia containing information completely compiled by users. Some people claim that allowing anyone to contribute leads to inaccuracy. Others point out that mistakes in Wikipedia are quickly corrected by others, and that the background discussions and history of how an article developed are always available for users to view.

Another type of collaboration is called "social bookmarking." Delicious and Digg are two examples where users share their online discoveries with others and provide keywords, called "tags," to make their favorites more accessible to others.

Some sites, such as Facebook and MySpace, exist solely to provide users with a place to interact with one another and form communities. A user sets up a personal page and profile, accumulates online "friends," and updates his or her page with short status messages highlighting what's important to them at the moment. Friends interact with one another by commenting back and forth on one another's pages, or using a multitude of other applications to stay connected. Other sites, such as Ning, provide a platform for people to form online communities where they develop a site as a group.

Web 2.0 users are not only involved with uploading or adding content to the Web. They also can get involved in software development, taking material from two or more applications to do a "mashup," combining them to produce a new application. For example, Google Maps are frequently used for mashups to pinpoint sites from another application. Mashups of video clips with pop songs are prevalent on YouTube.

This shift in focus from one-way, static communication to interactive, collaborative online communities brings with it a new set of issues. In this book, several are explored. The first chapter focuses on positive and negative aspects of online communities. The second chapter examines privacy issues that have risen from the sharing of personal information that happens in a Web 2.0 environment. The final chapter looks at how enticing these online communities can be, sometimes consuming huge amounts of time and distracting people from their daily lives. It remains to be seen whether there will be a Web 3.0, and if there is, what it will be like.

# Online Friends
and Community

# Making Friends in the Blogosphere

*Susan Olson*

*Susan Olson is an ordained Presbyterian minister. In this view-point, she talks about how blogging has provided a community for her, particularly with other female clergy. She describes how blogging communities develop and how she became an avid blogger. Her blogging community has been a source of friendship and support. She notes some of the positive characteristics of a blogging community—helping those who are geographically iso-lated to find support, providing a place to discuss sensitive issues without breaking confidentiality, being able to write a quick post without spending time editing—and some of the downsides— blogging to the extent that in-person relationships are neglected, problems with false information and slander, and the risk of ex-posing private issues.*

I never meant to start a blog. But one day I was reading Real Live Preacher (reallivepreacher.com) and followed one link to another link, then landed on a page where a woman was describing how she told her young daughter that a beloved congregant had died. She wrote with graceful prose and a few pinches of well-timed humor. On another site, a preacher discussed fingernail polish, evoking a spirited conversation about whether or not the well-dressed clergywoman should wear bright colors in the pulpit. Several pages discussed reactions to the PBS documentary film *The Congregation*. The conversations were lively, funny and tender. I kept reading.

Blogs, unlike informational Web pages, are interactive. In comment boxes following each post, readers can add to the conversation by typing in a few strokes at a keyboard. I was a lurker at first, reading the posts and the responses from the sidelines. Eventually, however, I left a comment, and then another. I began checking back to read how others had responded to what I'd written, and then I read the blogs of other commenters. I was hooked. A few weeks later I had a blog of my own, a pseudonym and a small network composed mainly of fellow women clergy.

Since my career straddles ministry and academia, my blogging network expanded rapidly to include a large number of professors and graduate students. Soon it was out of my hands. Today my blogroll (sort of a blogging posse) consists of a cadre of stay-at-home moms, computer specialists, musicians and expatriate grandmothers. Most evenings I spend time at the computer checking up on friends, composing posts and finding more gizmos (booklists that link to bookstores, word-of-the-day links and other features) to put on my blog page.

## Blogging Basics

For the uninitiated, blog is shorthand for Web log, or online journal. Several platforms, or technologies, are available on the Internet to help one set up a free or low-cost blog site.

There are as many blog topics as there are bloggers, but certain bloggers congregate together, regularly reading and commenting on each other's blogs. Correspondences develop, and these can become online friendships. Most pages include a blogroll, a list of links to other blogs that the writer enjoys checking regularly. Visitors can click through and meet the bloggers' friends and acquaintances. When I read a new blog, I often check out its blogroll.

Estimates of the number of blogs range from 3 million to 30 million, but no one knows for sure how many there are. This is because there is no uniformly accepted definition of blog, and no way to determine what constitutes an active blog. Since software and Web space are generally free, there is little incentive to remove an inactive blog even if one is no longer maintaining it, so discarded blogs live on in cyber-space.

## A Blogging Community

I spent my first ten years after divinity school in places where there were few other clergy of my age or gender. Not having a peer support system was hard in those first bleary-eyed years of ministry. I was unabashedly jealous of divinity school class-mates in more populous settings, and coveted their clergywomen's groups and their lunches with mentors. The shift from the ready-made divinity school community to the isolated existence of a 20-something college chaplain was rough. What a difference my new online community would have made back then!

It is a community. We pray with and for one another. We offer advice and hold one another accountable. When trouble hits, we respond. Every day I check the blogs of a second-career Methodist seminarian and a new Episcopal priest some-where "out there" in Montana. I eavesdrop on conversations between a stay-at-home mother and her four-year-old; I ad-vise a southern-lawyer-turned-Christian-educator on what to look for in a mother-of-the-bride dress. A midwestern clergy-woman writes about officiating at the funeral of a beloved church member; a West Coast counterpart presides over the closing of a church. A hospital chaplain's long-term relation-ship falls apart; a seminarian plans her wedding; a psychology professor is in love.

This is more than just voyeurism; these new friends share important aspects of their lives with me and enrich my life. Having a window into rural solo pastorates and urban store-front churches—ministries previously known to me only in the abstract—enhances my membership in the connectional church. The view into the particularities of denominations outside my own (and into my own denomination in other countries and regions) has widened my outlook.

Yes, I could read books or articles about these things, and I have. There is a difference, though, in learning through the personal narrative. It's like having a backstage pass to a performance you might have otherwise seen from the audience.

## Sharing Important Events

During the chaotic post-Katrina days, a pastor on the Gulf Coast suggested that we send books to her clergy friends who had lost their pastoral libraries in the storm. As a theological school administrator, I was able to ship 586 pounds of books to my friend to distribute. Another blogger went to Mississippi for two weeks to work as a supply preacher for beleaguered local pastors.

We share other life events. When a Virginia-based associate pastor announced her pregnancy, the blogging community congratulated her and offered advice on how to manage a pregnancy in the pulpit. A month prior to her delivery, over 50 bloggers presented her with a baby "blessing way." Each of us wrote and posted poems, prayers and good wishes. When my cat McKinley (my most cherished ordination gift) died, I received over 40 notes of condolence.

Some of the founding mothers of the clergy blogging movement are at www.revgalblogpals.blogspot.com. Here, 180 Revgals, some of whom are neither revs nor gals, participate in informal surveys, read weekly roundups (summaries of notable posts on member blogs), and purchase such delights as "Does this pulpit make my butt look big?" coffee mugs and Revgal-published devotionals. The community is growing daily.

I am not one of the founding mothers and am not active in the group projects (though I do love my mug). My involvement is limited mostly to my small base community, the bloggers whom I've enjoyed and befriended over the past year and a half. I have met some of them in person—at continuing-education events or when one of us has passed through the other's region. Others I will never meet and will know only by their pseudonyms.

At times I wonder if I can truly befriend someone when I may never hear that person's voice, never be with that person to share a meal or a laugh. At other times I remember a pen pal I had as a child, and relive the freedom of defining myself for that girl in South Dakota without the encumbrances of personal history or the interjections of others' opinions.

My letters offered my impressions of small-town Illinois life—and mine alone. If I wrote that the neighborhood ice cream shack's mint chocolate chip was superior to the down-town chains, it was. If I tried to be funny in my letters, I was—no neighbor or teacher was looking over my shoulder and recasting me as a serious, dreamy type. I experience that same freedom in blogging. If I say a sermon flopped, I don't have to argue about whether or not it flopped, but I can get feedback about how others have handled that sinking feeling while preaching.

Clergy isolated by geography, politics or demographics use the blogging platform to vent, to be vulnerable and to trust colleagues in ways that are appropriate and protective of pastor-parish confidentiality. Most do not blog under their own names and true locations, using pseudonyms instead. These give them distance and the freedom to think things through "out loud" without losing face or breaking confi-dences. It's easier to be honest about your concern for how your church will pay for a building renovation or how you'll replace a retiring organist if the "listener" doesn't know your name or state, and if you don't have to put a positive face on your congregation. Most clergy blogs also include references to issues in the blogger's personal life—dating worries, money woes, career concerns—that are uncomfortable or inappropri-ate conversation topics with congregants.

Blogging's speed is part of its appeal. You can jot down a post and not have to edit. Many bloggers write other forms of prose and view blogging as a writing exercise—quickly creating lots and lots of material without having to do much editing. Thanks to blogging, I've discovered a desire to write, to record my experiences without having to mold them to a particular audience or tie them to a particular scripture. When I applied for the Louisville Institute's Writing as a Spiritual Practice program, I submitted a revised blog entry. Having several "rough drafts" to choose from helped me meet a tight application deadline.

Blogging enables clergy and laity to be part of a community using slivers of available time. I can comment on three blogs in the ten minutes between work and an evening meeting, or write a post when I'm up at 3 A.M. with insomnia. Other blogs belong to clergy with children whose schedules are ruled by the twin dictators of vestry meetings and ballet lessons. Their social lives have shrunk.

## The Downside of Blogging

There is a downside. Some bloggers spend hours on the Internet and fail to cultivate outside relationships or interests. It is easy to get lost in the blogosphere and to wander aimlessly for hours. Most people's work and lives, however, demand that they limit such surfing.

Another downside is the presence of bloggers who propagate false information, or even use their bully pulpit to slander or malign. A year ago, a friend of mine was slandered regularly in a religious blog. When I wrote to the owner of the platform to complain, I was told that there was nothing the company could do about it, as blogs are considered opinion pages.

Perhaps the greatest risk of blogging is exposing private workplace issues. A young woman blogging under the name Dooce lost her job when her employers came across her written commentary on her workplace. Dooce's story is a cautionary tale ("dooced" is now a verb referring to losing one's job for blogging), and most bloggers take great pains to disguise sensitive topics, or avoid mentioning them.

Bloggers who avoid these pitfalls may find a rewarding experience in cultivating [an] online community. In the 18 months since I began blogging, I've become part of a virtual but real communion, one where I am a participant instead of a presider. This accidental congregation feels like church to me.

# Discouraging Online Friends

*John Lenger*

*John Lenger is an editor and journalism instructor at Harvard University. In this article, he lightheartedly outlines his reasons for not participating in social networking sites. He expresses his annoyance with e-mail solicitors and his concerns about the privacy of his "personal data" on social networking sites, concluding that he'd rather be friends with people in person.*

D ear friend (if I may still call you that): Recently I received an e-mail inviting me to be your friend on LinkedIn, Facebook, MySpace, Bebo, Friendster or some other professional- or social-networking Web site.

I receive many such e-mails, which I pretend I don't get. But LinkedFaceTickleFreakSpaceFriend, or whatever you call the Web site, keeps sending messages claiming to be you, so I feel compelled to respond.

I'm sure you mean well, and I'm flattered. But I'm not sure you've thought this through. At the risk of sounding un-friendly, this is why I can't be your friend:

1) Your friends may not be my friends. Your friends may be hyper-aggressive salespeople, spammers, stalkers, random jerks or just plain nuts. Not that I think your contacts are, but how do you weed out the weirdos online?

My e-mail and voice mail already overflow with demands from would-be friends that I buy their whirligig, hire their nephew or find a spot for their child in the next freshman class mostly from people I've never met.

If I joined you on BooBooFunnyFaceCookBook, or what-ever you call it, I would never have another moment's peace.

## Online Sites Share Information

2) You're a friend, not a revenue stream. When you send me photos, I frame them and display them in my home. When you post a photo, or anything else, on Friendster, "you automatically grant . . . to Friendster an irrevocable, perpetual, nonexclusive, fully-paid and worldwide license to use, copy, perform, display and distribute such content. . . ."

What a fun group! It gets better, though. On LinkedIn, you're not just a professional contact, you're "rich user profile data," all the better to sell to advertisers.

Facebook encourages advertisers to "pair your targeted ad with related actions from a user's friends." So you're hanging online with friends, and some giant, hungry Facebook spider is tracking your movements and selling that information.

Can it get any creepier than that?

3) Well, yes, it can. Once you give companies personal information, they can turn you into something you're not, as I learned making online purchases. Recently I signed onto eBay and was greeted with the message "John, fuel your passion for Male Nurse Action Figure!"

I bought my son a toy because he's interested in medicine. Now eBay thinks I want to meet guys in surgical scrubs.

Amazon.com thinks I need a subscription to *American Girl* magazine. I won't bore you with the hygienic product offers I get from retailers that have decided I'm not only female, I'm perpetually pregnant.

Not only is "personal data" the newest oxymoron, it's not even personally correct.

We already know that prospective employers Google your information on sites such as MySpace. I imagine networking sites could make quite a bundle by selling you back the compromising photos you shared in a moment of insanity, or better yet, charge to remove compromising photos from your profile that aren't of you.

4) Corporations used to become billion-dollar enterprises by owning stuff: airplanes, oil tankers, rain forests, that sort of thing. AOL bought Bebo in March for $850 million because it has . . . a list of your favorite 1980s bands and a photo of you doing the chicken dance at your cousin's wedding?

I don't want to ruin anyone's economy, but if the whole social networking boom is built on your performance of "Being With You," then dude, it's doomed. And then what happens to your personal data? Snapped up in a fire sale by an ISP [Internet service provider] in Uzbekistan?

5) Most important, friendships should be real, not conducted through a proxy such as MissingLinkSausageFaceSourPickle, or whatever it's called. Media hype would have you believe everyone is Facelinking, but a recent press release from The Conference Board puts the percentage of social networkers at 25 percent of those online. Seventy-five percent of us still like talking to real people! Alert the media! Or better yet, just give me a call. I'm always happy to hear from you.

# Online Friends Can Support You in Achieving Goals

*Keith Ferrazzi*

*Keith Ferrazzi is the head of Ferrazzi Greenlight, a strategic relationship consulting and professional development firm. In this article, he discusses how online friends can provide a support system to hold people accountable to achieving their goals. In particular, he describes a Facebook application he has created called Goal Post, where people can post goals and invite their Facebook friends to support them as they work toward their goals.*

What is the one thing parents, teachers, and bosses all have in common? Aside from the power they have likely wielded over you at some point in your life, these people have been responsible for an incredibly important task—holding you accountable. Whether it was your mother making sure you followed through on your chores or your second-grade teacher ensuring you did your own homework, you knew that someone would be checking in on you.

But now you're an adult, and the expectation is that you are supposed to brave this crazy world on your own and hold yourself accountable. Sadly, this is not always the case. We tend to be our own worst enemy when it comes to accountability, constantly making excuses and selling ourselves short for why we cannot or did not achieve our goals. For example, if you're anything like most people, you probably kissed your New Year's resolution goodbye around mid January and have a plethora of reasons why things "just didn't work out."

Now, who said goal setting had to come only once a year? Was it the same person who said you had to stop letting others hold you accountable?

Here's my suggestion: When it comes to setting and, more important, achieving your goals, do not do it alone. Setting goals often—and then meeting those goals—provides motivation and momentum that can lead you to bigger and better places. And having others hold you responsible makes you more likely to succeed. Too often, we fail at life because we lack a clear vision or plan about what we really want. We start to pursue a goal, but at the first sign of failure we give up. That's when an accountability group saves the day.

Since founding my company, I have always wanted to create a research branch to substantiate the work that we do. Whether I was too busy with another area of the company or a particular client, I never took the time to follow through on this goal. Finally I enlisted the support of my staff and my board to hold me accountable for starting this long-desired research institute. I set aside the time and resources to develop the institute because I knew so many others were now expecting me to make good. If I started to stray, they would put me back on course with encouragement and honest candor, which pushed me past my excuses and toward action. Now I have successfully launched the Ferrazzi Research Institute to bring cutting-edge research findings to our clients—forever changing the way we do business.

## Forming a Facebook Support Group

You are probably thinking, Gee, Keith, that's fantastic ... for you. I'm just too busy to make sure my friends hold me accountable. I will refrain from calling you a "quitter" and will suggest a simple solution: Facebook. Luckily for you, technology makes creating and managing an accountability group easier than ever. Why not leverage the power of your P2P [peer to peer] networks and use them for your benefit (as opposed to just killing time browsing for [dates])?

Earlier this year [2008] I launched a Facebook application called "Goal Post." The application allows you to set one or more goals, select friends to hold you accountable, and update your goal completion status as time goes by. Your accountability group is integrated into the process, and even non-accountability group peers can provide encouragement, inspiration, advice, techniques, and best methods while you are on your way to the top.

But who should be in the group? When selecting your accountability "buddies," try to choose people who will be honest, committed, and encouraging. Although Mom has always been great at nagging you, she might not be the best buddy because, to her, you will never be too fat, too ugly, or too stupid. However, that brutally honest friend may also be a poor choice because, to him, you will always be too fat, too ugly, and too stupid.

One idea is to target peers who are skilled in the area related to your goal. If your goal is to get fit by summer, your pal who is ripped beyond belief might be a good start. Another strategy is to partner with someone who might be seeking your skills—that way, you can benefit from each other while being motivated to keep each other on task. Additionally, selecting a friend with whom you have frequent interactions is important, as it is easier to lie about your progress to your cousin in London than it is to Nancy your next-door neighbor, and lying gets you nowhere fast.

So what are you waiting for? Go get buff for beach season. Find Prince Charming. Commandeer that job promotion. But whatever you do, don't try to do it alone.

# Making Virtual Friends on Facebook

*Peter Sagal*

*Peter Sagal hosts National Public Radio's* Wait, Wait . . . Don't
Tell Me! *In this transcript from the radio show* All Things Considered, *Sagal compares communities formed on social networking sites such as Facebook to the television series* Seinfeld. *He
describes the show as depicting four friends, none of whom are
particularly likeable, who continue to remain friends week after
week, and compares the show to social networking sites such as
Facebook, where friends keep track of what their friends are doing.*

Ten years after it went off the air, *Seinfeld* remains one of
the most popular comedies on TV. I think I can explain
this but I got to work my way around to it.

Recently, a friend of mine told me in great sadness that
Western civilization is coming to an end. The final sign of the
apocalypse? The social networking site, Facebook.

I found his view slightly extreme, although I think I can
sympathize. There's something vaguely creepy about all these
people friending each other online. There is something vaguely
creepy about using the word *friend* as a verb. Will this trend
spread? Will we be saying things like, Bob in accounting stole
my Cheez Whiz from the break room fridge so I enemied
him. Plus, why would anybody need or want hundreds or
thousands of friends? Groucho Marx said he wouldn't want to
be part of any club that would have him as a member.

But in my life I've taken that one step further. I don't even
ever ask to join a club because why give them the chance to

show their corruption by accepting me? No. Better to be a loner. A rock. A different drummer. I mean, to march to a different drummer, except I have no interest in hanging out with drummers. That's right. I'm such a loner, people, I am my own different drummer. Usually, I just tap my foot quietly, though, to avoid attracting unwanted attention from people I don't want to associate with. But nonetheless, recently, I went ahead and signed up for Facebook.

The gimmick of the site, of course, is that it provides you with constantly updated links telling you what your friends are up to. You'll notice a flaw, though, built into the system. You have to have friends to begin with. But it turns out it's actually a pretty good place to make friends. I found that a number of people I knew were already on it and I, yes, friended them. Pretty soon, I had a whole bunch of homies to hang with, virtually.

Okay, back to *Seinfeld*. The show had a tremendous amount going for it—terrific writing, some great performances, a refreshing lack of sentiment. But I think the heart of its appeal was its depiction of friendship. Four people, none of them particularly admirable or charming or even very likeable, and yet they were absolutely inseparable. Everyday, it seemed, they found themselves in that restaurant, talking.

No matter what they did to themselves or each other, they'd always be back at the restaurant the next week. They never expressed any affection. They didn't have to. It was, to use the Web 2.0 term, a social network. *Seinfeld*, for all its posturing, was not a show about nothing. It was a show about everybody's secret dream, to have a group of friends who know exactly how rotten you are, but still would never leave you.

A week after I joined Facebook, I had 100 friends. Now, I have close to 900. I check on them everyday. I will confess, I don't actually know most of these people. They seem nice, though. And it's a comforting thought that when I post things or mention what I'm doing, they find out. It's all virtual. They're not really there, of course. But it's still very comforting to think that no matter what I do, they still won't really be there tomorrow.

# Facebook Does Not Work for Me

*Joe Lavin*

*In this article, Joe Lavin explains why he does not like social net-*
*working. He describes how his Facebook account, created three*
*years before, still only has four friends. He is selective about ac-*
*cepting friend requests, especially from people he does not*
*know—although he avoids using the "ignore" button, fearing he*
*will hurt their feelings. Lavin also says he is too much of a pri-*
*vate person to want to use the status bar to post what he is do-*
*ing. So, he has decided to post his status as "not accepting friend*
*requests at this time." Lavin's writing has appeared in numerous*
*publications. He publishes a weekly online humor column.*

Here from the relative safety of the printed word, I would like to announce that I am a failure at Facebook. I've had a Facebook account for three years now, and I have a grand total of four—count 'em—four friends. That's an average of just over one new friend a year. You have to be either incredibly discerning or incredibly unpopular to fail so magnificently at social networking.

I first visited Facebook three years ago not because I was ahead of the curve, but because I worked in the same office as the guy who founded the site. I was working in a Harvard department, and he was an intern there.

Truth be told, I always thought he was a little too smug for a 19-year-old kid. In retrospect, though, it appears that I was a little too smug for someone who was not about to become an Internet millionaire, and he was doing just fine on the smugness scale.

I created an account, but then let it lie dormant until [2008] when my girlfriend joined. She convinced me to revive my old account, and, for about 48 hours, I loved Facebook. I soon had added all four of my friends. I looked up people from high school. I searched for dirt on people in my department. I put up pictures, wrote on people's walls, and even sent people free gifts.

There was even some romance when I officially entered into a relationship with my girlfriend. Here's how the wooing worked: First, I sent her a friend request, and then she added me as her boyfriend. Facebook then asked me if I accepted her request. I did, and we were suddenly boyfriend and girlfriend.

Wow, is that how it's done these days? As a typical commitment-phobe guy, I have to admit I was a little nervous about clicking "confirm" on her boyfriend request.

This would, of course, have been a beautiful moment that we would treasure forever, except that I accidentally dumped her five minutes later because I didn't know what I was doing.

Fortunately, after playing the field for a few minutes, I figured things out and began dating her again. Our relationship is much the stronger because of it.

Unfortunately, though, my interest in Facebook soon waned. While I'm only 36, Facebook makes me feel old. I fear that I don't get social networking. For example, I have this apparently odd habit of accepting friend requests only from people who are, like, friends—you know, people I have met before and whose company I enjoy.

As you are no doubt thinking, such a notion is almost Victorian in its quaintness. I might as well write letters to people, too.

This, of course, is why I have only four friends. And when you have so few friends, there are other problems. By accepting my next friend request, in some ways I will be designating that person as my fifth closest friend online. And that's just a little too much pressure to put on a friendship. So far, no one else has quite made the cut.

It seems especially odd when I get a friend request from someone I don't know. Why do people I have never heard of send me friend requests? Cass, Dave, Ryan, and Beth, I'm deeply sorry. I've never met you before, but thanks for the friend requests. Rest assured that they are still on my entry page, mainly because until recently I was so dumb that I thought you would find out if I rejected you.

I knew there was an "ignore" button, but it seemed a harsh way to treat a stranger. All this time, I have instead been manually ignoring these friend requests. Manual ignoring is something I have always excelled at, and I am reluctant to hand over the controls of my ignoring to a computer. I'm old-fashioned that way.

In some ways, I'm just not an open enough person to be on Facebook. The status line where you tell everyone what you are doing right now terrifies me.

First of all, you don't need to know what I am doing right now. And I especially don't like that my status will be instantly broadcast to all my friends. OK, there are only four of them, but you get the point.

And even if I did want to broadcast my status, you always have to put something witty there so you seem interesting. Look around and it appears that everyone has a snappy line. "Joe Lavin is at work," or "Joe Lavin is writing a snarky article about Facebook" just won't cut it.

To be accurate, next time I think I'll just put up, "Joe Lavin is not accepting friend requests at this time."

# Sharing Experiences Through a Blog

*Paulo Coelho*

*In this article, best-selling author Paulo Coehlo talks about several ways that he uses the Internet, particularly his blog, to interact with his readers. When travelling in remote areas of the world, he carried on conversations about his travels through his blog. He has distributed free electronic copies of his books online. In addition, he has asked readers to help him with a film adaptation of one of his books, by filming scenes from the book and posting them on YouTube and by posting ideas for the musical score on MySpace.*

The American journalist Jeff Jarvis has come by my house to interview me. Here I am, face to face with one of the most incisive technology journalists of today—via his blog BuzzMachine—and he is asking me what I think of the internet. I find the idea mind-boggling, to say the least; it would have been unthinkable a decade ago, when Google was a fledgling search engine and the internet a mystery to most of us.

Still, I had a suspicion at the time about the potential of this new medium, and I decided to launch my own website and newsletter, and opened an email account for readers who wanted to contact me. One of the myths about writers is that we write our books in lonely ivory towers; in my case, I was never very keen on the notion of the reclusive author working in solitude, and have always tried to interact with my readers.

So I've spent a lot of time on my website, knowing that it is one of the rare public platforms, besides the traditional book signing, open to me. Yet, despite the success of the site and newsletter, I felt that more could be done—but what? The answer is the result of ten years' fascination with the medium.

## My Virtual Journey

In 2006, I decided that, rather than separate myself from the world, I would take a different path. The road is made by walking—this is the first tenet of every adventure. You place your foot on uncharted terrain and from there the road somehow imposes itself on the walker. I left my house in France for three months, visiting Tunisia, Italy, Bulgaria and Ukraine, before I embarked on my Trans-Siberian journey, a 5,772-mile trip from Moscow to Vladivostok.

I shared my experiences every two to three days with readers from all over the globe via my blog. The feedback was incredible—despite my being in this remote region, I wasn't alone: people were travelling with me through my words. The blog lasted a couple of months; I knew, though, that this first contact had to evolve somehow. But how?

When I returned home, I had a couple of months before the publication of my novel, *The Witch of Portobello*. I knew from previous experience that the free-sharing of my book over the internet would increase its visibility, so I didn't hesitate to post it on peer-to-peer websites and on my blog.

The more I've ventured into the virtual world, the more I have realised that the internet has a logic of its own and its credo is: share everything freely. This was my message when I spoke at the "Digital, Life, Design" conference in Munich earlier this year [2008].

The feedback from readers and media alike to the internet incarnation of *The Witch of Portobello* was such that I started a blog called the Pirate Coelho, where I posted links to free electronic copies of my books. Of course, this "underground" activity was undertaken without the knowledge of my publishers. But on the official side of things, I was also exploring as many ways as possible of communicating with my public via websites such as MySpace, Facebook and YouTube.

## Collaborating on a Film

Then, one day [in 2007] in Geneva, after visiting the blogs of some of my readers, I had an idea: why not work together? From this simple thought emerged the Experimental Witch project. I extended an online invitation to participate in a film adaptation of *The Witch of Portobello*. Aspiring film-makers were asked to film one of the 13 tales that the book inter-weaves and post the results on YouTube. Musicians could use MySpace to send ideas for the soundtrack.

Now, the submissions are all in, and the winning entries will be announced on my birthday, 24 August [2008]. Though some excellent work may be left aside in arriving at a manage-able length for the film, this distant collaboration means I have been able to see the film my readers picture as they read my work.

So I looked at Jeff after he'd finished his questions, and asked him: "What else should I do?"

Apparently, Jeff thinks I'm doing just fine.

# Using My Blog to Promote a Cause

*David Rothman, interviewed by Michael A. Banks*

*David Rothman is the founder of TeleRead, an organization devoted to creating a national digital library of electronic books (e-books). In this interview with Michael A. Banks, Rothman talks about how he uses a blog as a tool to promote TeleRead. He describes the successes he has had in being recognized by other bloggers and the news media, and some of the financial challenges he has faced by not accepting advertising on his blog. He works to provide information and provoke discussion on his blog, rather than merely using his blog as a form of online press release.*

*[B*anks:] Did you start blogging as an extension of promoting your cause?*

[Rothman:] Yes. I started TeleRead.org to promote the cause of well-stocked national digital libraries and related matters, especially e-books. The e-book–focused blog happened because no one also was covering the issues—technical, legal, you name it—in the depth and manner that I wanted.

I'm also interested in stimulating people to provide answers to problems, in a collective process.

*Are you achieving what you set out to do with the TeleBlog?*

TeleBlog is doing its share, and it is achieving visibility. It helps that we're included in many blogrolls, including the Wired Campus blog of the *Chronicle of Higher Education.*

TeleBlog has been a leader in the area of e-book standards, [which are] very important to the future usability of e-books. E-books aren't going to really become as popular as, say, CDs

Michael Banks, "David Rothman," *Blogging Heroes: Interviews with 30 of the World's Top Bloggers.* 2008, pp. 56–59, 61–62. Copyright © 2008 by Wiley Publishing, Inc. Reproduced with permission of John Wiley & Sons, Inc.

or MP3s until there is a standard. And I'm talking about one the big publishers are comfortable with, as opposed to simply distributing e-books in ASCII or HTML. That's why John Noring and I started OpenReader [www.openreader.org]. I doubt OpenReader will end up being the final standard, but it has influenced the thinking of the International Digital Publishing Forum [www.idpf.org], and they have taken e-book standards a lot more seriously as a result of OpenReader, which arose from TeleBlog.

Our traffic is pretty good for a specialized site. It's hard to pin down the number of readers because many read us on RSS. The number of unique visitors per day is typically in the region of a thousand. But there are times when the accesses are well above one thousand. We are interested in sponsors, but they have to be people who won't try to influence the content of the site in ways that could be very harmful to our credibility.

Again, though, please understand I didn't start TeleRead to make money. The talk about donations or other support is simply a matter of sustainability. We have avoided appeals for small donations except for a quick experiment with an Amazon tip jar.

*How much time do you think you spend on the blog?*

It can vary all over the place. Sometimes it'll be just a few hours a day. Sometimes I'll just bang out something and focus on a book or whatever else I might be up to.

But some days—and this is where I need badly to find the right business model—sometimes it can take up most of the day, or a working day and then some.

As I've implied, for now the blog is financially a disaster. But the operative words are "for now." I'm convinced that something good will happen. If nothing else, possibly the LibraryCity project will work out, and that can be a source of income for me and for others.

*What is your source of inspiration for postings? Do you read many other blogs?*

Basically I combine news items with my years of writing about e-books. and come up with connections that might elude other people. I get some great ideas from readers, but basically I do a lot of surfing and a lot of RSS-ing.

As for other blogs, I look at them directly and I follow them through RSS feeds. I have hundreds in my reader. I'm not claiming to read every weekly item from the hundreds of blogs I follow, but I'll read RSS on my desktop, I'll read it on my tablet, I'll read RSS even on my Palm TX PDA.

My ambition is to be in a position where I'm reading fewer rather than more feeds. I'd much rather be reading books than RSS feeds. This is the way in which the blog is a time sink, in that you can't do a good job without keeping up with the rest of the world, and that takes time. But the mainstream people don't care sufficiently about e-book-format standards and other important topics. And more than a few are clueless on topics such as draconian DRM [digital rights management]. So I work to bring information to the public.

*Do you have time to do much posting on other blogs?*

I do occasional posts, and every now and then I attempt to get slashdotted, but I generally stay within the confines of the TeleBlog, because I feel that I have so much to cover for the blog that I just can't take time out to be all over the net.

I know it sounds hypocritical, but because the blog has become such a centralized hub for the e-book world (it's not the only one out there, but it's one of the major sites), people are posting not only in their home blog, but also coming to us with some real gems. I love it when they share. And they in turn get greater exposure in most cases. I figure that by tending my own little garden, I can better fertilize the ground for other people.

*What do you do to bring in new readers?*

I'm not doing anything special to attract readers, other than trying to provide a quality site and blog. Normally, readers and the media just find me. This a concern for me. I'm very frustrated that I can't clone myself, so that one David can do the blog and the other promote it.

I have been fortunate to have gotten media attention over the years. I get quoted in publications like *Newsday*, and I've been mentioned on the National Public Radio (NPR) website. In the past, TeleRead has been included in the *New York Times* site list, and the *Washington Post* has linked to TeleRead.

Ironically, I'm often outdrawing http://libraryjournal.com, according to http://alexa.com, although neither of us would be in the big leagues. . . .

*What do you think of the blogging world at large?*

I see bloggers as being able to assume a unique role in the scheme of things. Some blogs try to provide news, to function just like a newspaper, though usually specialized. But I see a different potential for bloggers, a role in which bloggers raise questions. But a blogger typically doesn't have the time or resources to get the final answers to those questions. This is where traditional journalism comes in, to answer those questions.

Yes, it's true that bloggers have "answers" in terms of their opinions, but in terms of answers on specific issues, there ought to be a synergy between the mainstream media and the blog world.

Not a lot of bloggers appreciate how much energy is involved in news-gathering for the mainstream media. It's true that you can get a lot of information from documents. I did reporting, for example, under a grant years ago from the Fund for Investigative Journalism, and a lot of my work involved interpretation of documents. But that is not all that's involved in gathering news. A lot of what the media does involves interaction either over the phone or in person with newsmakers. And because most bloggers blog in their off hours, they're not going to have the same interaction with newsmakers that members of the mainstream media have.

On the other hand, the members of the mainstream media are so busy gathering news that they may lack time for reflection, and they may be so interested in immediate details that they fail to connect the dots.

But if a synergism is established, the media will notice the questions raised by bloggers, and some good hard news stories will result.

So I'm not just interested in providing answers. I am interested in stimulating people to provide answers themselves, in a collective process, though I'd like to think that the Tele-Blog is practicing journalism. Its just not traditional journalism in the sense that the coverage is influenced by the cause.

I see some blogs that are nothing more than disguised outlets for news releases, and this is unfortunate, as those blogs could be offering fresh information and raising questions.

I also have to say that, as a group, the major e-book and publishing-related blogs, and others associated with publishing and writing, tend to be better than blogs as a whole. This is true not just in the writing, which is to be expected, but in the overall organization and quality.

And there is the integrity issue. If I find adverse information about e-books, I'm going to put it in the blog. In fact I *want* to put it in the blog, so people can think about answers—whereas a lot of people who might have a cause to advocate will let that limit the kind of coverage they do.

*Do you have any specific advice for other bloggers—to do a better job, to attract readers, whatever the positives may be?*

My biggest advice is to work to get people information that is relevant to them. Don't just come up with arguments; provide information along the way. It's a way to reward people for the time they spend visiting your blog. A newsy approach is always better than a static, pamphleteering one.

# Online Dating Can Be Deceptive

*Fred Gonzalez*

*Fred Gonzalez, a columnist for the* Miami Herald, *has some qualms about online dating. Friends suggested many online dating sites for him to consider. When he started browsing the sites, all the profiles looked the same to him. As he began meeting women in person that he had contacted online, he realized that profiles also could be deceptive. He describes his experience in the following article.*

Online dating has become a staple in the singles world, with sites running the gamut from one-night affairs to religion-based coupling.

When I found myself back in the dating game, the online choices were overwhelming. Which service should I use? Friends had different opinions, debating the finer points of Match.com vs. eHarmony.

No, try AmericanSingles, one would say. Or PlentyofFish, it's free. What about Yahoo personals or MySpace?

As I cruised through the sites, the photos started to look the same, and the profiles read identical.

Nearly every woman I clicked on in the 25-to-33 age bracket was searching for someone with about 22 qualities that must be met: You need to be spontaneous and ambitious, not into games, and you better know how to enjoy a Blockbuster night at home or you are toast.

## Profiles Can Be Deceptive

Now, to be fair, I am sure there are some classic men's profiles out there, detailing the number of cars and boats at their various houses, how many times they visit the gym and a listing of attributes (perhaps mostly physical) that they seek in a partner.

The profiles all seemed to omit any negatives—I figured it was just people accentuating the positives to make a good first impression. But once I chose a site to sign up with, I quickly realized how deceptive these profiles can be.

Why do we try and be something we are not when trying to attract potential dates? Are we doing it in order to be what we think someone else wants? That's easier to do when we can hide behind the computer screen. But there's no hiding when you finally meet in person.

One of the first dates I had was with a woman who claimed to be 5-foot-4. When we met at a bar for some Grey Goose La Poire and appetizers, she was already sitting on a bar stool.

The conversation was snappy and the date went well. When it was time to leave, things changed. I moved forward to finish paying the bartender, and when I turned around, she was nowhere to be found. But she hadn't left; I just had to look down. There she was, all 4 foot 10 of her, ready to stroll Las Olas Boulevard. I hate to sound mean, but it looked like I was on a Big Brothers, Big Sisters outing. For me, it was a deal-breaker.

The next "date deception" came with a woman who contacted me first. That's a rarity in my online dating world, so I couldn't pass up on the flattery. I should have known something was up from her photos on her profile. They were a bit, uh, fuzzy. When we met for a drink, things came into focus.

We shook hands, and all I could do was stare at the receding hairline. Not the waiter's. Not the bartender's. Hers.

Talk about awkward. It was so prominent that it was hard to keep from asking about it, perhaps encourage her to try some Rogaine. Thankfully, I stopped myself. But when my

"Operation Eject" text message came through from a friend, we split the bill and left. (Still the fastest date I have ever had.)

To be fair, I am sure guys don't always measure up to their profiles. Receding hairlines are just the half of it.

CHAPTER 2

# Privacy Issues
# with Web 2.0

# Life Is an Open Book on Facebook

*Kelly Roesler*

*Writer Kelly Roesler was nervous when she first joined Facebook. She had heard a lot about Facebook, and many of her friends had joined before she decided to sign up. In this article, she talks about her Facebook experience. She begins by describing the main elements of a Facebook page. She goes on to describe what she sees as Facebook's benefits and pitfalls. Benefits include keeping updated on friends' lives and finding old friends and acquaintances. Pitfalls include getting friend requests from people she did not like or even know, learning more than she wanted to know about friends' relationships, and getting caught in the middle when friends saw who else was on her friends list.*

I remember feeling strangely shy and nervous, my heart pounding in my ears, the moment I joined Facebook, the hugely popular social networking website, several months ago.

I knew little about it, but some of my closest friends had become members and urged me to do the same. It was generating major buzz, mainly as a word-of-mouth phenomenon. I'd received many e-mail invitations to join, most of which I ignored.

Eventually, after a few of my most trusted friends took the leap, I followed suit. I created my free-of-charge Facebook profile and posted it, unsettled by its mysteriousness and worried I might be in over my head. I had many questions: what does this involve? What kind of people do this? For what purpose? Would I find many friends? And what would happen when I found them?

Facebook, I knew, had begun as a virtual yearbook for university and college students, but grown to include anyone with an e-mail address. Still, I wondered, what was the point?

## A Facebook Page Layout

It was immediately clear to me that a Facebook profile page acts as a window into a member's life.

The pages are designed in a clear, modular layout to convey as much flowing information as possible in a readable format.

At the top of the page is a lárge profile picture of the member, flanked by personal, self-confessed details such as age, marital status, political and religious views.

Below is a mini-news feed, documenting a person's recent Facebook activity—whose "wall" they've written on, who they've become friends with, new features they've added to their profile and "status" changes.

To the left side of the screen are thumbnail pictures of a member's Facebook "friends"—his or her chosen inner circle—with a link to the full list of friends. For many, clicking from one friend's page to another to another has become the new great Internet time-waster.

In the centre of the page, there are spaces left for contact information and as much personal information as one wants to include, from favourite music, books, movies and quotes to employment and education details.

Below and to the left, there are spots for links to photo albums, posted notes and groups the member has joined.

Toward the bottom of the page is the "wall," where friends publicly post comments and messages that can be viewed by anyone looking at the page.

The unique format has proven to be one of the most successful of its kind, with an appeal that stands apart from similar websites such as Friendster, Twitter, MySpace and Class mates.com. There are 145,136 Facebook members in the Ottawa [Ontario] network, with 23 million worldwide and growing.

Accordingly, Facebook Inc., supported by advertising, harbours an ambitious strategy for expansion, recently inviting tech companies and programmers to create features for the service, permitting them to profit from this. For now, Facebook won't take a cut.

The new features allow Facebook users to recommend and listen to music, add book reviews to their pages, play games and more, without leaving the site. Until now, Facebook users were limited to making online connections, sharing photos and planning events.

But Facebook has a huge vision for the future. Mark Zuckerberg, its 23-year-old chief executive, has said the company is positioning itself as a "social operating system" for the Internet, its eye on an eventual lucrative acquisition or a public offering. But not just yet—it was reported that [in 2006], Facebook turned down a $900-million U.S. acquisition offer from Yahoo! Inc.

Meanwhile, rumour has it that Facebook could be on its way out, the cachet spoiled by its increasingly mainstream appeal (and by the growing number of parents creating profiles to keep tabs on their kids).

## What Facebook Is About

And yet it really wasn't that long ago that I finally clued into what Facebook was when I signed on, after months of wondering.

Was it an unending quest to amass a list of as many friends as possible so as to appear popular and important? Was it a convenient medium for self-promotion and advertising? Or is it a valuable new way of interacting, allowing us to build relationships with those around us and rediscover people we thought we'd never meet again?

For me, it's been all of the above. Facebook can be whatever a user wants it to be. Key, however, to a great Facebook experience is to be aware of how to use it, all its possible pitfalls and problems and how to maximize the benefits for you (and have fun) without compromising your dignity or privacy.

Facebook offers tremendous voyeuristic thrills. As a newbie, I was immediately overwhelmed at the wall of information and news feeds updating me on my friends' daily activities, bombarding me as I logged into my home page. But it made for fascinating reading.

I could find out what my friends were up to at that precise moment, what mood they were in, what events they planned to attend, their ever-changing relationship status (Facebook offers several options to choose from, including "In a relationship" or "married," to "random play" or the laughably desperate "whatever I can get"), and peruse their personal photo albums, posted notes and every virtual move, down to the minute.

I still play Facebook's great game, scanning my friends' lists of friends for familiar faces. And if someone belongs to the Ottawa network, I can, in some cases, view his or her entire profile without adding them as a friend.

Yes, all I saw were words and tiny pictures on my computer screen. But I was nonetheless riveted by the unexpected drama. Some friends sent thinly veiled messages through their status updates. "Down and out again, wish I could wake up to a new life," wrote one. An out-of-town friend wrote about her homesickness. Another posted updates on his pending child custody case; another wonders why his eye is bleeding.

Heart-shaped alerts happily informed when a friend had paired up with someone. A broken heart went out to signal to everyone in that person's network that the relationship has soured, pinpointing the very time it happened.

One day at 12:45 *p.m.* I learned my good friend Doug was "now in a relationship." By 2 *p.m.*, my news feed was stamped with the demise of his relationship: "Doug is now listed as single." Humiliatingly, this went on for another few days, and before long, Doug announced he was cancelling his Facebook profile—to no one's surprise.

I read profiles with interest, keen to know the literary, musical and political tastes of others. Facebook users can band together in groups, and I carefully looked for those with interests close to my own. Many of my groups are related to journalism, the art of writing and music. Others are purely for fun ("The Jason Spezza fan club" and "Wish I was in New York City!")

## Adding New Friends

Every time I received a new "friend request" by e-mail, I was thrilled. Was it a kindred spirit from work? A long-lost friend? Perhaps a family member? But my excitement soon dwindled after I received request upon request from people I barely knew or had lost touch with—for good reason.

Through Facebook, I found old friends, romantic partners, acquaintances and colleagues, including some who, as I've learned, may have been better left in the past. I was surprised to get requests from several members of a former friend's family—which I did accept, to be greeted by silence.

For some, the bar for Facebook "friendships" is set low. I've had requests from people I know to see, or vaguely remember having passed in the hallway at school, yet can't recall ever having a single conversation with (a pattern that's since continued on Facebook).

I joined a group for former students of my elementary school to receive requests from people with whom I attended kindergarten. It was exciting—for a time. After the initial "what have you been up to?" messages were exchanged, conversations and the contacts petered out with nothing more to sustain them.

Of course, it wasn't just who was "friending" me through Facebook that made me feel awkward. Sometimes, bizarre interactions would ensue.

For instance, the ability to look at your friends' list of contacts can pose problems. I discovered this when one person, a close friend from college with a casual attitude toward Facebook friending, tried to add one of my work friends to his contact list. The two had never met. I soon had a quizzical message from my "work friend" who wondered why he had done this. In the end, it resulted in tense conversations with both friends, and I seriously considered cancelling my account.

Facebook's recent partnerships with companies that create applications that can be added to users' home pages certainly add to the information a member can reveal. Quite possibly they go a little too far in the process. The applications allow users to share their favourite music, books, movies and videos, and have included rating systems to rate the "hotness" of the Facebook member on their profile, and, more bizarrely, the "honesty box," which asks viewers to reveal their "true" feelings toward their Facebook friend.

Not only do these seem to beg for trouble, they've transformed the typical Facebook profile page from a simple, uniform, clean design to a cluttered, colourful and overwhelming mess—recalling the problems that plague MySpace.

While I've become somewhat disillusioned with Facebook after a period of rather heavy use, I've also become addicted to the constant flow of news about the people surrounding me. It's the second website I check every morning. I love learning everything, even the most minute details, about the people I know and to have one more way to communicate with them.

Facebook's element of suspense and excitement are undeniably attractive. But I've struggled to find a balance when it comes to my own profile and the information I'm willing to share. I ask friends not to take my picture for Facebook sharing; I prefer to maintain control over my photos. I agonize endlessly over what information I should post. It took me a long while to weigh the consequences of revealing my love of punk music and my affinity for David Lynch films. I've removed my wall posts—the platform for friends to post messages—in order to preserve my privacy.

Finally, after several months, I think I've mastered the Facebook dance.

# Hoping My Dad Will Not Embarrass Me on MySpace

*Christopher Short*

*In this article, Christopher Short, an editorial assistant for the Colorado Springs* Gazette, *expresses his concern that MySpace should provide a place where young people can be themselves without their parents being part of their MySpace friends. Short's dad sent him a friend request on MySpace and he felt obliged to accept his dad's request. However, he wonders about the etiquette of having his dad as a MySpace friend, he worries about his other friends knowing that his dad is looking in on them, and fears that more of his family will also want to befriend him.*

A few years ago, the technology simply didn't exist for this kind of mortification.

It's enough to make a man long for the heady, carefree days of 2004.

See, today my dad got a MySpace account—and sent me a friend request.

I have a healthy social life, or at least you could get that impression by looking at my profile.

I am the proud owner of a robust three-digit friend total, not bad for someone who signs in only once or twice a week (and seldom leaves the house in real life—but that's a different column).

My point is that, Dad, who recently started qualifying for the senior meals at Denny's, should easily melt into the virtual throngs.

My friends with the melodramatic, language-challenged screen names will likely not even notice his presence.

In fact, I'm keeping his name to myself to ensure just that—don't go snooping, EtEr-NaL EmBrAsE.

Nonetheless, this feels like the broadband equivalent of taking an aunt to the prom.

## MySpace Should Be a Safe Haven

If there's a safe haven for youths, where kids of any age needn't fear the meddling of their elders, it should be MySpace. The tacky "pimped out" wallpapers, sparkly animated comments and auto-loading emo music should all but guarantee the exclusion of interlopers, right?

How exactly did Dad break through the ramparts?

Don't get me wrong: My dad is a great guy.

He's always supported me in everything I've done, well thought-out and otherwise.

He taught me to love the Beatles, and never made me try out for football.

When he visited a few months ago, my wife and I didn't pay for a meal or drink for a week.

Still, he's forcing the sort of "netiquette" crisis I haven't experienced since I skipped a bunch of psych classes and had to e-mail the professor to ask which chapters a test would cover (awkward).

Clearly I have to accept Dad's request, but am I also obligated to Top-8 him?

Sure, he gave me life, but what if he starts leaving embarrassing comments?

How do I tell him his emoticons are creepy?

And for that matter, where does the madness end?

I have one more parent, and two stepparents; two grandmas, and more than a dozen aunts and uncles.

Are all of them going to crash my virtual party, too?

Consider this an open plea to Tom, the MySpace founder, my first friend and yours: If you wish to protect whatever sanctity exists in social-networking Web sites, you must develop software that will screen out 'rents, or at least keep them from contacting their kids.

It may be too late for me, but millions of youngsters will certainly thank you.

In the meantime, if you'll excuse me, I have to go download the most obnoxious emo song I can find.

# Personalized Web Services Pose a Privacy Risk

*Becky Hogge*

*Becky Hogge is the Executive Director of the Open Rights Group, a grassroots digital civil liberties campaigning organization, and a writer for the* New Statesman. *In the following article, Hogge discusses how hard it is to keep your personal data private on the Web. She notes that most of the services she uses are Web-based, which was helpful when her laptop died and she did not lose all of her digital photos. The problem is that for each of those services, a user must log in, and most users use different information for each service. New projects that manage user log-in data have been developed, but this only increases the privacy problem, as there is only one password protecting a user's information.*

Last year when my laptop broke, I almost lost all my digital photos. The photos weren't on the computer—I use the online photo-sharing service Flickr. But I couldn't remember my Flickr ID and password; the web browser installed on my laptop had always remembered it for me.

In general, I'm happy that most of the services I use are web-based: Gmail for email, Del.icio.us for links, Dopplr, Facebook and LinkedIn for social networking—the list goes on. I may not be typical—I'm a geek, and that's why I get to write this column. But I'm indicative of what's to come. The web is developing from a place where we read stuff, through a place we interact with, into a place we personalise.

However, in order to personalise the web, we must first log in. And in order to use lots of services, we must log in lots of times, if we're sensible, using different passwords. Every service, shop and bank with which we interact online knows these logins and passwords, and uses that knowledge to establish trust that we are whom we say we are.

## Identity Providers

That puts the burden firmly on our shoulders, and the more identities we have online, the greater that burden becomes. This provider-centric approach is in the process of being challenged by new user-centric projects such as OpenID. OpenID seeks to set up a competitive market of identity providers, based around open standards that already exist on the web. In simple terms, that means that you only need remember one passcode—your OpenID provider assures all the services you use that you're the same person you said you were last time. And if you don't like the way your OpenID provider is handling your data, you can switch providers.

The scheme has been tentatively adopted by AOL, Microsoft, Sun, Novell and, more recently, by Google and Yahoo! It is now spawning even more user-centric approaches, such as ProjectVRM, which hopes to use OpenID to build a community of service users that can exercise real power.

But it's not just about logins. Last month when Robert Scoble, the *über*-blogger, was kicked off Facebook for trying to export data about his 5,000 friends to a rival service, he shone a spotlight on the issue of data portability. Soon, it won't be just our logins we'll want to travel with us as we roam around the web, it will be our photos, videos and friends, too.

At the centre of this debate are the twin spectres of security and privacy—however easy it is to carry around, if you've got all your eggs in one basket, you need only trip up once to find yourself eating the proverbial privacy omelette.

"People are going to voice concerns about privacy," says the data portability advocacy site DataPortability.org, "but soon enough the actuaries will insure our personal privacy, much like they do every other aspect of our lives." Until that day comes, it might be a good idea to continue spreading the privacy risk.

# Balancing Safety and Censorship

## Elizabeth Lane Lawley

*Elizabeth Lane Lawley is an associate professor of information technology at the Rochester Institute of Technology. In this post from her blog, mamamusings, she talks about the challenges of being a parent who supports her son's exploration of technology while at the same time wanting to keep him safe. She sees many positive aspects of her son's blog, where he writes about his thoughts and experiences, but she worries that he is too young to judge what personal information, such as his address and phone number, should be made available on the Internet. She worries about how to prevent some stranger's posting abusive or inappropriate comments on his blog, and how to keep other strangers from contacting him via instant messaging, without censoring everything her son does online. She does not draw any conclusions, but continues to try to maintain a balance.*

I've been thinking about filtering a lot lately. Much of that thought has been spurred by watching my kids—especially my older son—exploring social software. He's blogging now, and is reading my blog as well. He's an IM [instant messaging] wizard, enthusiastically working with far more open conversation windows than I can manage without my brain overheating. He hangs out in Neopets, and signs online petitions to allow fan sites to post Neopet photos. He does all this wirelessly from the hand-me-down Powerbook G3 that he got for his birthday this year [2004].

All good things, in theory. What's not to like for a parent who's as much of an Internet and social software geek as I am? Well—plenty.

Let's start with the blog. The benefits of his blogging have been multi-fold and inspiring—it spurred him to write enthusiastically and in detail about our trip to Asia, it made him aware that he had a platform from which he could explore not just his experiences but also his questions and frustrations (like book censorship, for example), it made his teacher (and his classmates, and their parents) aware of the power of student-generated content generally, and blogs specifically.

But with blog readership comes the inevitable blog spam. After the first few "enlargement" comments, I installed MT-blacklist, which helps a lot. But that's a short-term solution, since the ingenuity of spammers tends to outpace the rate of solution provision. The new MT comment registration service may help more—we'll see.

## Teaching Children About Privacy

But what's more challenging are the oh-so-difficult questions of public vs private information online. For example, *I* know not to put my home phone number and address on my blog. But he and his friends haven't yet developed those instinctive filters for personal information—and on several occasions, I've found our home number, along with those of his friends, in a blog posting. I quickly edited that out on the blogs I control—but it left me more than a little unnerved.

Recently, he and his friends discovered BlogSpot and decided to set up a group blog to complain about every child's favorite problem—their parents. Anyone with kids knows that good parenting isn't always popular parenting, but that doesn't make it any less painful to see one's children publicly reviling you for what they see as unfair and hurtful actions.

So we had a talk. He reads my blog, and complains (with reason, I think) if I talk too much about him. There are purists who would argue that if I were a *real* writer, I wouldn't allow his reactions (or anyone else's) to change what I write. But I do think about my audience when I write, and I think about how what I write will affect them and my relationship with them—now, and in the future. And I want him to do the same. "How do you think it makes me feel when you write mostly about what you think is wrong with me?" I asked him. I don't begrudge him his feelings, or his right to an outlet. But I do want him to understand that publicly expressing those feelings can and will have an effect on the people who read them. It was a good talk, a valuable talk. But it remains to be seen to what extent it changes his use of this exhilarating medium—and it also remains to be seen if my husband and I will continue to encourage this level of freedom of expression if we see it as putting him or his friends at risk.

## Broken Rules

And while we're on the topic of risk, there's that pesky IM thing. I walked into the room where he was typing the other day, and he quickly closed the IM window. My parental radar kicked in immediately. "Who were you talking to?" I asked. "Just a friend," he answered, intentionally vague. We eyed each other. I told him I really needed to know who it was, but that I didn't have to see what was being written. "Was it someone I know?" "No." "Who was it?" "He's a kid that T (a neighborhood friend) met online. He's 13."

*WHOOP! WHOOP! WHOOP!* (That's the sound of the all-hands-on-deck alarm that went off in my head.)

"We had a deal," I said. "IM *only* with people you already know in person, and not with anyone Dad or I haven't approved to put on your buddy list."

He protested, telling me that he could tell this was a nice kid, that he was smart enough not to reveal any personal information via IM, that obviously I didn't trust him or think he was smart. To no avail in this case—I'm not willing to budge on this rule, and I made that clear. But I'm deeply concerned—we had the rule in place, and he broke it. How do I know it won't happen again?

## Balancing Protection and Encouragement

So I'm caught. On the one hand, I want to encourage his exploration and use of online media and interaction. On the other, he's right—I don't trust him not to make potentially dangerous mistakes. It's not that I don't think he's smart, or savvy, or listening to my warnings. What he doesn't understand—what he *can't* understand—is how easy it is to be fooled, to be taken in, to be taken advantage of. *Especially* when you're honest to a fault, as he is—because it's that much harder to really understand just how dangerous and dishonest so many people "out there" can be.

(As an example of how this honesty plays out, here's what happened after we found out the boys had been visiting "NSFW" [not safe for work] sites on one of our computers—via a phone call from one of their friends' parents. I had a serious talk with them about appropriate use of the computers, and the risk of lost privileges. I told them that the computer recorded all the sites they went to, and that I'd be checking that on a regular basis. A day or two later, while I was at work, they came rushing downstairs to talk to Dad. "We accidentally ended up on a page that had grownup stuff on it, but it's okay. We left the site, *and* we erased it from the history of the browser so that mom wouldn't get upset!" He didn't know whether to be delighted at their honesty or dismayed at their obvious mastery of the technology.)

This isn't a new problem for parents. We all struggle with the "stranger danger" issues these days—how do we keep our kids from being paralyzed with fear at the sight of a stranger while still keeping them safe from the very really harm that lurks around too many corners? I don't have answers right now, just questions, and concerns.

For the time being, I'm continuing to err on the side of access, with a healthy dose of oversight and communication. But I'm also hoping that better solutions for children's use of technology begin to emerge. A kids' IM client that I can configure in terms of access, for example. An easy to install and configure weblog client that lets me approve posts before they go live. Varying levels of access that I can allow or remove, depending on each child's activities and maturity. I wish I saw more work happening in this space, though I understand that COPPA [Child Online Privacy Protection Act] makes it difficult.

# Learning About Students' Lives on Facebook

*Julia Goode*

*Julia Goode (a pseudonym) is a professor at a midwestern law school. In this article, she discusses being Facebook friends with her students. As a professor, she kept her Facebook persona professional, treating it as an extension of her other communications with students. She enjoyed learning about her students' lives in this way, although she tried not to be intrusive. She notes, however, that there are times, especially when grades are posted, that students need a place to vent about their professors, and she regrets that her presence on Facebook limits the amount of venting they can do there.*

I'm getting dangerously close to feeling old—well, maybe not old, but definitely not young. When I began my teaching career, I wasn't that much older than my law-school students. But the gap widens with each passing year, and I am definitely minding.

I've heard other professors express the same sentiment. You tell a joke in class about an event that seems as if it happened last week—the Iran-contra hearings or the O.J. Simpson trial—and you get blank stares in return. You quote from movies you are certain everyone has seen, and, sure enough, no one in the classroom has. You end up feeling about as cool as an eight-track tape deck and as old as the hills.

So when I noticed that my sisters-in-law, who are in their early 30s as compared with my late 30s, had created pages on Facebook, I was determined not to be left behind. I had read in a newspaper article (online, of course) that really cool young people didn't e-mail one another anymore, they "face-booked." I didn't know what that meant, but I was ready to advance to the next instant-communications level.

I threw up a fairly simple profile page, complete with a picture of me and my youngest child ("See, I'm not really old and fat; I'm merely postpartum and sleep-deprived!"). I filled out the basic information—where I work, where I went to school, where I live, and marital status. I declined to spend the next 20 hours of my life providing information on my favorite books, TV shows, movies, political leanings, and quotes, and I didn't add any plug-in games, quizzes, or surveys.

I may be technologically advanced for my age, but I do have a real job that takes up some of my time.

Once my profile was live, I invited my sisters-in-law to be my Facebook "friends." They graciously accepted and congratulated me on being so technologically savvy. They wrote messages on my "wall" to the effect of "Welcome to the 21st century." I felt very hip.

But then something quite unexpected happened. My students found me.

## Students as Friends

At first, just a few asked me to be Facebook "friends." When their friends saw that they were friends with me, then those friends asked me to be their Facebook friends, too. Soon I was "facebooking" with half my class.

I am neither ignorant nor risk seeking, so my Facebook persona quickly emerged as an online representation of my classroom persona. My status updates ("Julia is [fill in the blank].") reflected what was going on in my classroom or in the life of the law school. When students wrote on my "wall," I wrote back with the same tone, language, and substance as I would if I were responding to an e-mail message from them or a question in the hall. Conscious of my audience, I didn't add family photo books or political campaign slogans.

I was comfortable with my appearance in this new arena. I thought of Facebook as nothing more than an interactive office door. I was wrong.

First came the realization that, although I was a mere professor on Facebook, my students were much more than students there. When they looked at my profile, they saw basically the same version of me that they would see if they looked around my office or sat next to me at lunch. But when I looked at their profiles, I saw everything about their lives. And it was fun.

I noticed that they liked to make fun of their professors. I cracked up at their spot-on parodies of my colleagues' mannerisms and figures of speech, and was flattered to see that my own eccentricities were sufficiently interesting to become fodder for their parodies.

I also noticed how tight-knit my students were as a group. They talked about going to parties and meeting for lunch, and they seemed to be really great friends. They posted pictures from student events and videos of themselves dancing. I remembered the great study group I had when I was a student in law school and how I thrived on spending 12 hours a day with such clever, witty people, all of us trying to survive the same law-school traumas.

I was glad to see that my students had each other to keep them afloat while legal education tried their souls. During finals, they wrote words of encouragement on one another's Facebook walls and issued self-deprecating angst reports in their status lines. I began to enjoy reading their status updates as if I were watching a real-time, legal version of [popular TV series] *Grey's Anatomy*, only with characters I knew who were a lot more lovable than the ones on the show.

Facebook is like a giant reality show. I unwittingly became privy to the ups and downs in my students' relationships, job hunts, and vacation plans. I could see which television programs they watched and which movies they liked. I tried not to look that often, but occasionally a student would see me in the hall and yell, "Hey, look at my new pictures on Facebook! I've got a funny picture of Professor Z at the awards banquet." Yes, and several pictures of you dancing with another person in our class, I notice.

Students began using Facebook instead of e-mail to communicate with me. When the dean announced that I had been promoted and approved for tenure, my students wrote on my wall to show their support.

So maybe I was receiving too much information about their private lives. But I thought the additional insights would only help me guide students and be a better mentor.

## Facebook Reactions to Grades

But then I turned in my grades for the spring semester, and the reality show we were all starring in got to that uncomfortable, tense point at which you want to leave the room or change the channel. Students who did well in the course used Facebook to "message" me to say how much they loved the class. Students who received low grades changed their status lines to reflect their disappointment.

This was the side of grading that I never had to see. I normally turn in grades in December or May, and by the time I see students again, the next semester has started, and they have moved past the grades they received in the previous term. Maybe a handful of students drop by to look at their exams and ask why they received a B+ instead of an A−. But most of the students who earn low grades from me never cross my path again; only rarely do any of them register for another of my classes.

But this semester, in Facebook land, I was seeing their elation and disappointment in real time. The students also seemed to know that I was there in cyberspace, and that knowledge added to their discomfort. They may have been

been tempted to use Facebook as a way to tell their peers about how completely unfair my exam was and how much of a witch I am.

That is not only their right but a rite of passage. Venting frustration by taking it out on the professor is cathartic and can be healthy—if not taken to obsessive extremes. With the magic of Facebook, disappointed students should be able to write on one another's walls: "Professor Goode is such a tool!" "What do you expect from such a freak of a professor?" "That class was such a waste!" Instead, knowing I might be watching, my students censored themselves and used code phrases: "I am having such a bad day." "I am here if you want to chat!" Our Facebook friendship seemed to rob them of the ability to cope online.

I hope they were able to remember how us old folks had to grieve over grades. We just got everyone together in the same bricks-and-mortar room and kvetched [complained] about the professor, school, and life in general, usually accompanied by lots of fattening foods (among other things).

So I am reminded that just because I'm Facebook friends with twentysomethings, I'm still the old crone that has to hand out a few less-than-average grades to some of them twice a year. In a matter of weeks, the crisis will pass, and life on Facebook will return to normal. I'll just be the professional friend who posts something funny on her interactive office door every once in a while.

# A Celebrity's Perspective on MySpace

*Alec Mapa*

*When celebrity Alec Mapa first started visiting MySpace, he found someone was impersonating him by starting a MySpace account under his name and leaving comments on other people's pages that were supposedly said by him. In order to combat this impostor, Mapa started his own MySpace page. He now spends countless hours down what he calls "the MySpace rabbit hole," observing the lives of noncelebrities. Mapa is an American actor, comedian, and writer.*

At first I was flattered that someone was impersonating me on MySpace with a fake Alec Mapa page. Then it just got creepy. Particularly when the ersatz Gaysian began posting comments on other people's pages like "You're hot!" or "Let's get together!" or my favorite, "Pee on me!" While those sound like things I'd actually say, I didn't write them. So I narc'd on the imposter, posted a genuine page of my own, and I was immediately sucked into the gay vortex that is MySpace.

I am by nature an extremely nosy person. MySpace is like a gigantic international queer medicine cabinet I can snoop through for hours. I click on your profile, look at pictures of you and your boyfriend in Mykonos, read your blogs and comments, click on your friends' profiles, lather, rinse, repeat. I fall down the MySpace rabbit hole for hours, logging off only when the red-hot glare of my infuriated and neglected husband burns through my skin. I'm the opposite of a celebrity stalker. I don't care if Brad ever leaves Angie for Jen or if Britney ever finds her panties. I am, however, dying to know which guys from King of Prussia, Pa., slept with each other at

Gay Days in Orlando. I eavesdrop on conversations. I'll read a comment on someone's page like "It was so great seeing you too. It's been too long. Don't be a stranger" and then click on the person's profile to see what prompted the exchange in the first place: "Thanks for not stealing anything. I like you so much better since you've stopped doing crystal." I even write people who write me. Then giggle when they think I'm an impersonator. It's the perfect pastime for an insomniac.

On one of my many late-night snoopfests, I came across a poem about cutting written by a young gay man living in the middle of Texas. I've never cut myself per se, but I completely recognized my own self-inflicted wounds in his spare, heart-breaking prose. It was so well-written I left a message telling him how much I enjoyed it. He wrote back. He told me he was raised in the Bible Belt, surrounded by cotton farms. To him, being gay meant furtive, hasty Senator [Larry] Craig-like trysts in roadside toilets—a late-night anonymous mauling in the shadowy recesses of a truck stop. Not seeing himself happy in any of those scenarios, he joined an "ex-gay" ministry group in Dallas. After every single meeting of reparative therapy and prayer, he would cut himself bloody with a stainless steel razor blade. On the weeks he missed a meeting, he wouldn't. He'd attend another meeting and start cutting himself again. He stopped going completely and hasn't cut himself since.

Ironically, it was the ex-gay ministry group that facilitated his coming-out process. "First of all, it was in Dallas. I'd never actually seen a thriving gay community outside a television show or newspaper article. For all I knew, it was just propaganda set in place by the 'gay agenda.' Second, I worked in a home decor chain that's very popular with gay men. I was outed by the staff before I fluffed my first beaded pillow." He now lives as an out gay man and travels all over the country competing as a blocker in the North American Gay Volleyball Association.

We still correspond from time to time, dropping each other an occasional comment or message. I'm not sure either one of us is wholly convinced that we are the people we say we are, having never actually met. But that's the great thing about MySpace. You can be anyone you say you are—unless you're pretending to be me. That's, just weird.

# YouTube Advertisements Are Invasive

## Jonathan Jacobson

*Jonathan Jacobson likes surfing YouTube, but he has some concerns about advertising. In this article, he discusses how advertisers track usage on YouTube and other sites in order to provide advertising on YouTube that is targeted specifically for the person. Jacobson was a student at the University of Illinois at Urbana-Champaign when he wrote this article.*

On a recent night over winter break, I was sitting alone in my room surfing YouTube. Of course, this is nothing out of the ordinary. But it is amazing how quickly things can turn strange when you're alone in your room and it's late at night.

So, as I was saying, everything was going fine. But then it happened. And I must say that I was surprised, if not disgusted. It was something I had been waiting for, something I had been afraid of for too long. Sort of like a new installment in the Rambo franchise. But this, to be sure, was absolutely worse.

On my little YouTube screen, at approximately 2:37 *a.m.*, a pop-up advertisement appeared and blocked a small portion of the video I was watching. I knew at this moment that things were going to be very different from now on.

To the average person, this is not a big deal. Most would merely let the little rollover ad block the screen for a few seconds and then go back to watching some kid beat Super Mario World in seven minutes flat. But I could not resist clicking on the pop up. After all, who doesn't want to know why Cingular can save me more money than Sprint?

Clicking on the advertisements on this new feature—YouTube rolled out the service, called InVideo Ads, a few months ago [in 2007]—will actually pause the video you are watching while the new ad plays on top.

## Advertisers Track Internet Use

The problem here is not immediately obvious, which is generally the case for most small annoyances in our lives. It is easy to avoid these ads. They only block the lower fifth of the screen and, even then, only for a few seconds. And you, unlike me, don't have to click on them. The problem is an underlying one.

Google, which owns YouTube, has developed new and, frankly, frightening ways to allow advertisers to access the exact market they want at all times. Even at 2:37 *a.m.*, when most advertising executives are snug in their 1,000 thread-count sheets, advertising software is checking my e-mail for me to determine that I need, by way of example, a hip T-shirt and a freelance job.

Even if this were the case—and I'm not saying it's not—I am uncomfortable with inanimate computer programs tracking my desires.

After consulting with my brother—who is a business major at this University [of Illinois] and a far less finicky person than myself—I determined that I am nothing if not a walking market segment. A potential customer to the world's commercial interests. This is, apparently, what they are teaching in the business school. The world has now become, for all intents and purposes, an enormous shopping mall that I can never escape.

And all I wanted to do was entertain myself for a few minutes before bed.

This issue is nothing new. Advertisers have long been trying to extract information from the Internet and tailor their message to a specific target. YouTube was hardly a year off the ground when the "world chief creative officer" at Leo Burnett, the most prestigious ad agency in the world, touted the video-sharing site as a greater potential source of revenue than MTV.

This guy's job title—which, by the way, could only exist in the modern world—is part of the problem. Creativity, in the advertising realm, is now equated with finding me in my pajamas, silhouetted by the warm glow of my monitor, and telling me the things that I want.

I certainly don't believe that every ad exec is Scrooge McDuck, poised ponderously at the end of a diving board above a pool of gold coins in his money bin. My concern, as usual, is on a far grander scale. Put simply, I don't like to know that people and machines are watching me.

These new InVideo ads are only a symptom of the greater disease, for which there is only one cure: lock yourself in a room and cover your head with tin foil. That way they can't get you.

# Using Facebook for Snooping

*Jen Gerson*

*Writer Jen Gerson has used Facebook to snoop in the lives of her ex-boyfriends, former classmates, and everyone else she has ever known. In this article, she describes some of her Facebook spying and talks about the general lack of discretion in a society where detailed personal information and photos are posted on the Internet and there is no longer a distinction between private and public spheres. Gerson has written for a variety of newspapers; she won a National Newspaper Award for short features in 2006.*

I found him on Facebook.

He's chubby now, sports a cubic zirconia in one ear and a thin beard trimmed tight around the jaw. For religious views, he writes "SMOKE WEED EVERY DAY." Favourite books "hahahahahahahahahaha. Who has time to read?" He says he's an exotic dancer at Chip & Dales where he works "as eye candy for money."

This is the guy who tormented me in high school.

He called me a dork. He reminded me daily of how few people liked me. He accused me of being a lesbian in biology class.

His Facebook profile has become a source of constant comfort. Whenever I feel disliked or dorky, I look at his page. His lack of success in life fills me with petty glee.

Unlike others in Generation Y, I use Facebook for more nefarious purposes than just keeping track of my acquaintances or inviting people to parties or sharing photos. I am a shameless snoop. I use it to spy and I'm not afraid to admit it.

Myspace, Facebook and now services such as Twitter are reconnecting us with every person we've met since childhood.

I know where the person I hate most is working. I know who my Grade 4 choir rival is dating. I know that a high school friend with a baby is addicted to eBay.

I've looked up all of my exes.

Facebook claims more than 430,000 members in Toronto—a number that, following a Gladwellian Tipping Point [referring to Malcolm Gladwell's book *The Tipping Point*], has almost doubled in the past month—it's a trend that's not likely to blow out. The Internet has made it easy to keep up and keep snooping. It's turning us—not just me—into a generation of voyeurs.

Facebook can act as a party planner, and then provide the virtual space to upload evidence of the debauchery. It allows for moment by moment updates with blog-like authority. The amount of detail on a Facebook page can be overwhelming.

"You can be a Facebook stalker," says Spencer Vaudry, 18. "It gets ridiculous."

Of course, the impulse to spy would be nothing without a cadre of bloggers, bookers and exhibitionists ready to sate the demand.

One of these is Justin Kan, 23. The San Franciscan attached a video camera to his head almost two weeks ago and has broadcast the minutiae of his life in real time on Justin.tv. Initially he included his cellphone number so fans could call him, but eventually had to remove it.

"My cellphone has physically exploded because of call volume."

Kan also dealt with pranksters who called 9-1-1 on him, bringing armed officers into his home—one of the more dramatic moments of an Internet phenom that includes more mundane moments; such as Kan eating, Kan sleeping, Kan using the bathroom . . .

"Why am I doing this? Because it's a lot of fun," he says. "I get to show people what it's like to live the life of Justin Kan. And people have liked it and that's a pretty good feeling."

Five hundred people watch Kan sleep.

Feeding the Internet the details of our lives is addictive. It makes every party we go to, every fight, every insight feel like they are worth publishing. It makes our lives seem grand and theatrical.

Break-ups between friends and lovers are no longer just gossip, they are sent via RSS feed to the inboxes of our followers, also known as friends.

I don't think any of us can make a clear distinction between the private and public spheres of our lives anymore. Is it okay to upload drunken photos of ourselves on the Internet if the album is private? Can we blog about our jobs if our Livejournal doesn't attach our name?

We understand anonymity and permissions and privacy settings, but know nothing about discretion.

Pundits have been warning us for years that these indiscretions will come back to haunt us; that our drunken rampages and open drug use will keep us from finding jobs; that our advertised one-night stands will scare away potential mates.

I'm less worried about this than I am about a generation that thinks nothing about putting video cameras on every street corner. I'm worried that we're making ourselves vulnerable to government and corporations who will use our indiscretion to quietly wrest our privacy from us.

Facebook makes me worried about a world in which no one needs to watch us, because we're all watching one another.

# Web 2.0 Consumes
# Daily Life

# Already Too Connected

*Leah Rumack*

*Journalist Leah Rumack signed up for a Friendster account in 2003, and was satisfied with her online Friendster identity and relationships. Soon, friends started leaving Friendster for MySpace, and encouraged her to set up a MySpace account, which she did. Next, friends wanted her to join Facebook, which began as a social networking site for college students only and opened up to the general public in 2006. In this article, she protests that she does not have time for yet another online life. Rumack is a pop culture journalist who has written for the* Toronto Globe and Mail, National Post, *and* Fashion, *among other publications.*

We are the dissenters, the online resistance fighters and the conscientious objectors of our day. And I have one thing to say—*we refuse.*

I dreamt about using my BlackBerry last night. And I don't even have a BlackBerry. Nor will I give in to that bullying bunch of ne'er-do-wells who've been digitally harassing me. They are trying to make me join Facebook. And it's not just me they're after.

"I joined Facebook," confessed one of my friends, burying her head in her hands in shame. "I did it. I cracked."

We thought we were safe. Facebook was the one online networking site we thought was reserved for the youth of today—a place where bat mitzvah [the Jewish rite of passage for young women] girls posted their spring break pictures (and honestly, ladies, when I was a bat mitzvah girl, we didn't get up to such sordid business). It started out as the domain of university students and teenagers but, [in 2006], Facebook membership was opened to the public, and now everyone I know is breaking. Suddenly, the number of e-mails urging me to join Facebook, sent by my supposedly grown-up-and-busy-with-jobs friends, has gone from a trickle to a flood.

"What's the matter with you?!" I hissed at the first hapless losers who tried to get me to join. "Don't you know that site is for kids?"

First it was Friendster, then MySpace, and now this. Where will it end?

Social networking sites—for those of you who have been ossifying under an electric typewriter—are online communities where you can post a profile listing things like your relationship status, interests and, frankly, fantastic musical tastes. These are then linked to profiles of friends, favourite bands and random men from Nigeria—"Hello my darling. I am Afansz. I love you!"—who decide they want to be your friend, and you let them because you are bored. I tell two friends, they tell two friends, and so on and so on, like some endless Finesse shampoo commercial or some viral marketing popularity contest.

Urban hipster kidults—those of us in our 30s who still live like we are 25, but with nicer apartments and better taste in wine—have long been communicating, dating and networking on these sites.

## Satisfied on Friendster

Innocently, I joined Friendster in 2003. I added friends and pictures; I acquired new friends and dates, I found out about upcoming events; I helped people find jobs. So when MySpace became the thing and everyone started jumping ship like a bunch of fair-weather floozies, I held out with the sort of righteousness I now reserve for Facebook.

"I'm already on Friendster!" I protested. "I have a life, you know."

But I eventually gave in (or so I like to think) because part of my job involves writing about music, and bands would increasingly refer lazy journalists to their MySpace pages for information (instead of spoon-feeding it to them as they did in the olden days) and you had to be a member to view them. And also, I couldn't be all not cool and on the wrong networking site—that would just be lame.

"This is it," I told myself. "No more online lives!"

But the endless perfecting of this non-interaction-with-actual-people is turning me into a rabid, typing shut-in with a bad case of carpal tunnel and a slightly grey pallor. Case in point: I can barely understand the phone any more.

After years of e-mailing, MySpacing and Friendstering, the telephone, as a device for actual communication, seems hopelessly retro. So much so that I was actually flummoxed by the bizarre habit of an erstwhile beau of mine, who, sick to death of e-mail, began using the phone machine just to talk. Note: He wasn't text messaging, and it wasn't a quick call on his cell to come meet him at a bar. He was calling the actual phone. In my house!

The phone machine would jangle, interrupting my seamless e-mail prose and the curating of my most recent MySpace pictures. I would stare at the machine, confused, as it screeched like some paleolithic harridan [nagging woman] teleported from 1991. Hadn't we already made plans for tomorrow night? What does he want? What is the phone machine doing? Is it my mother? Is someone trying to buzz up to the apartment? "Hello?" "Hey! It's me." "Um, yes?"

Recently, another friend told me that a certain gentleman had inquired after me and he'd given him my phone number.

"You gave him my phone number?!" I said, shocked. "What kind of man actually calls a woman and asks her out? What is this, 1957? Have you never heard of MySpace?"

Clearly, I need help. I will not join Facebook. I will not. But I don't feel safe. I just got an e-mail from a friend with the cheery tag: "Allison wants you to join Twitter!"

"Hey, Leah," she writes, "this is way more fun and simple than MySpace and Facebook and all that crap. It's fun! And addictive! Check it out! Come on!"

You know what, Allison? Call me on the damn phone.

# Twitter Is Not Just a Waste of Time

*Becky Hogge*

*Twitter is a social networking site where members participate a number of times each day, answering the question "What are you doing?" in 140 characters or less. Members "follow" the posts of other Twits and receive updates either online or on a mobile phone. Writer Becky Hogge was skeptical about joining Twitter at first, wondering, what was the point? After participating for a while, she discovered that getting quick updates on the minutiae of friends' lives helped her stay connected with them in ways that seeing them in person did not. Becky Hogge is executive director of Open Rights Group, a grassroots digital civil liberties campaigning organization.*

"Emergency. Not enough Sunday left—do I install new software, write my column, or take down the Christmas tree?" Just a few short weeks after [Nobel Prize–winning author] Doris Lessing condemned the inanities of "the internet," I joined seemingly the most inane group of internet users out there. Although Twitter has been around [since 2006], you may not have heard of this social networking service. Unlike Facebook, there are no zombies, no online games of Scrabble, and no one-click facility to arrange birthday drinks or leaving parties. Twitter asks one simple question "What are you doing?" The task of the Twitter user, or "Twit", is to reply in fewer than 140 characters, several times a day, no matter how boring your life is.

"Feeling overfull. Really nice salmon cakes downstairs, but they didn't feel so filling until I got back to my desk!" I had been a Twitter refusenik since I noticed that the geekier of my friends had started getting more SMS [short message service] messages than me. Twitter, you see, crosses the web/mobile divide, letting users opt to receive updates from their network of Twitter friends and contacts on their phone, in real time.

What could be the point of receiving a text message letting you know that your colleague has overcooked his spaghetti? Or that your favourite blogger is stuck in a European airport with no good wifi? Yet after a few months, such questions became so burning, that even I had to join: "Yay, the boiler man has just fixed the boiler. Now I can go out."

Twitter was co-founded by Evan Williams, the man who sold the blogging platform Blogger to Google. Back then, most people thought blogging was inane and pointless, so it may follow that in a few years' time we'll all be tweeting on Twitter (or similar sites, like Jaiku and Pownce). In a recent article for MIT's *Technology Review*, Elizabeth Lawley, director of the social computing lab at the Rochester Institute of Technology, described its appeal: "The question 'What are you doing?' is exactly the thing we ask people we care about." It's "almost as if you're seeing a pixel in someone else's life".

"Bloody hell, it's awful out there. We are staying in, cooking a tagine and listening to music. Feels like a Sunday." After a week on Twitter, I'm coming round to Lawley's point of view. I get a chance to meet up with each of my friends properly (ie, in a pub) about once every two months. By then, there's so much to catch up on, that the small stuff gets lost. Bumping into a girlfriend a few days into my Twitter experiment, I find we are smiling about my Sunday Christmas tree conundrum and her bad pizza last week. The events may not be newsworthy, but the shared knowledge of them brings us closer.

So I'm sticking with Twitter. It may not be as revolutionary as blogging, but so far, it's fun. "Finished my column: off to have veggie curry in Stroud Green." A twit's paradise.

# Obsessed with Reading Blogs

*Lucy Sweet*

*Scottish author and musician Lucy Sweet loves reading blogs of people she does not know. There are several people she follows every day and she wants to know everything about everyone she has not met. In this article, she talks about how at one time this kind of behavior would have earned her the label of "stalker," but blogs allow her to indulge her obsession without actually invading anyone's privacy.*

Excuse me, have you done a blog? No, it's OK, no need to buy a plunger—I mean an online diary detailing every tedious moment of your boring life?

Well if you have, chances are I'll be hovering in cyberspace watching your every move.

It's not something I'm particularly proud of, but I lurk around in blogs more frequently than [singer] George Michael.

I can't help it. I want to know all about people I've never met, and every day I obsessively check a handful of diaries by my fake "friends" who in real life would slap a restraining order on me before you could say "blog off".

## Four Favorite Blogs

I've got four blogs I can't get enough of and no diary entry is too humdrum to stop me poking my nose in.

One is by a woman in Chicago called Mimi Smartypants, a sassy, loud-mouthed gal with a daughter called Nora and a cat named Bananas.

Then there's LA-based artist Kime Buzzelli who runs her own shop/gallery, a bloke called Dave who is a long-haired tour manager for minor league indie bands, and a girl called

Alicia who makes handbags and muffins and lives in an obscenely cosy Martha Stewart-style pod of domestic perfection.

I have no idea who these people are or why I care about their little projects and observations about the weather. I'm not even sure I'd like them if we met.

For example, the other day Alicia made chicken tikka masala from scratch for an Indian-themed night, which was inspired by a delightful embroidered smock she bought on eBay. Barf.

I'm sure a psychologist would say the lives of these strangers represent my own aspirations and desires.

Deep down, instead of sitting on the bus wondering whether Johnny Depp is going to dump Vanessa Paradis and come and live in my airing cupboard [clothes closet], I crave adventure and excitement.

I want to make perfect muffins, have a cat named after a piece of fruit, live on a bus with smelly rock bands and put on cool, hipster art shows in LA.

## Wanting to Know Everything About Everyone

But the truth is I'm just incapable of minding my own beeswax. I don't care who you are—I want to know EVERYTHING about you.

People like me used to be put on government registers. Now, though, thanks to the interweb, there's no such thing as privacy and us lurkers can happily scour the insides of people's heads, look at their holiday snap[shot]s and drool over their homemade chicken tikka masalas without any pesky court cases or ASBOs [anti-social behavior orders] getting in the way.

If the internet didn't exist, I'd be hanging over the garden fence hitching up my left boob with my elbow like [comedian] Les Dawson and gassing about the price of fish.

My nosiness knows no bounds. So much so, I want everyone who does a blog to send me a link to it so I can live my life through you and find out what you had for tea last Thursday.

Just call me an "interested observer". (*Stalker* is such an ugly word.)

Of course, these bloggers bring it on themselves. If Alicia, Dave, Kime and Mimi are going to use the internet as if it's a five-year diary with a little gold lock on it, then they deserve all the weird, creepy blog botherers they get.

Most other people keep their innermost thoughts to themselves and hide their diaries in knicker [underwear] drawers until they die, when relatives read them, realise there's nothing juicy and chuck them in the bin [trash].

Let's face it, apart from Elton John and Keith Richards, most of us are dull as Hull [a UK city]. So it's amazing that blogs exist at all, knowing how samey [alike] human beings are.

Personally, I would never be so self-obsessed and arrogant to bore the world about all the stupid things I get up to every week. Oh. Hang on a minute, I already do.

# Hooked on Social Networking

*Jade Wright*

*In this article, musician Jade Wright talks about what she calls her addiction to MySpace. She has over three thousand MySpace friends, most of whom she has never met. She enjoys reading their profiles, chatting with them, and learning about their lives. She compares MySpace to the television show* Big Brother, *where for a short time she gets hooked on observing someone's life, until, a few weeks later, she has forgotten about them.*

I've developed a really bad habit. I sit wasting hours, when I should be in bed, in front of the computer poring (although thankfully not pawing) over pictures of strangers.

No, it's nothing untoward—I'm just hooked on the world of social networking sites.

I'm beginning to understand why 16- to 25-year-olds are spending more time watching their computers than the telly [TV] and why Facebook, which lets users upload a personal profile including a real name, photograph and interests, was ranked in a survey of students in the US as their third favourite thing—behind beer and iPods, but above sex.

I wouldn't quite go that far, but user-generated content is quite breathtakingly exciting, as the [Liverpool] ECHO office seems to have discovered this week. We've been going MySpace mad.

Surely this isn't healthy. For one, my line between online and real world interaction is beginning to blur. Of my 3,000 MySpace friends, I must have met less than 1%.

The rest could be anybody, but then I like that. Chatting to odd people over the world appeals to my hippy upbringing.

## MySpace Is Addictive

As my sensible friends ask me, what is the point of spending a big chunk of my evening staring at a computer screen when that is precisely what I've been doing all day? But then it's so incredibly addictive.

These sites have millions of members using their personal page to e-mail and post bulletins, blogs and photos of themselves.

With one click, you know what someone looks like, where they live, how old they are, whether they're single and what star sign they are, whether or not they plan to have children, but also their favourite bands and often which gigs they'll be at. It's stalker heaven, the ultimate in people watching.

It's like Big Brother in your own home, with no rationing if you're naughty and fewer surgically enhanced people hoping to get a photoshoot in *Nuts* magazine.

Talking of *Big Brother*, I'm far too excited about the coming series. Yes, I know it's passe and a bit rubbish, but I can't help wanting to squeal every time I see the big eye flash up between programmes on Channel 4.

I know that come next weekend I shall be hooked to every row and burp, that I'll have my favourites and the ones I passionately dislike and that a few weeks after it's all finished I'll have forgotten them all. It's rather like chewing gum—disposable, tacky and rapidly becomes tasteless.

Bring it on I say. I'm just glad it doesn't get stuck on my shoe.

# Addicted to MySpace

*Rob Alderman, as told to Candice M. Kelsey*

*Rob Alderman is a graduate student from Tennessee. He was one of the last of his buddies to start using MySpace. In this viewpoint, as told to author Candice M. Kelsey, he describes how he set up his MySpace profile and soon began to feel addicted, adding friends, adding comments to other people's pages and waiting for them to add comments to his. At one point, his was among the ten most-read blogs on the site. After deciding MySpace was becoming an addiction, he decided to take a two-week break and gain some perspective on his life.*

I've been having trouble beating my addiction. I've tried and tried, but it seems like I will never be free. It's the first thing I do when I wake up in the morning, and the last thing I do before I go to bed. I do it at least twelve times a day, sometimes more. Curse you MySpace—I hate your guts.

I remember when I was the guy who wasn't doing the MySpace thing. Not being much of a computer type, I just couldn't see what all the fuss was about. All of my buddies kept bugging me about it though, and so I thought to myself, 'Well, it wouldn't hurt to try it once.' I went through the process of making a profile, entering in all of my information in great detail, and then came the photos. Grabbing my phone, I quickly snapped a picture that looked just right for MySpace: black-and-white, not looking directly at the camera, with just a hint of melancholy. Perfect. Finally, a name. I had to be careful, because MySpace kept warning me that once I had chosen one, it couldn't be changed—ever. With that finished, I clicked 'Submit' and held my breath.

## My First MySpace Friends

It was a life-changing moment when I saw the words for the first time: 'You have a friend request.' Soon, I was adding friends and requesting to be friends with people I'd never met. As my list of friends grew, I quickly became aware that I would have to be very careful about who was in my coveted 'Top 8.'

I was writing blogs, reading blogs, commenting on blogs, commenting on comments, joining groups, creating groups, posting bulletins, reading bulletins, taking top ten quizzes that told the world what I thought about my favorite CDs and movies, and what character I would be if I was living in the world of Buffy the Vampire Slayer! My greatest MySpace moment occurred when one of my blogs cracked the top ten most-read blogs on the site. Not bad, considering MySpace then boasted over forty-five million subscribers. Suddenly, people I had never met were posting comments about my personal life.

But in the back of my mind there were faint alarms going off. What exactly is it that causes us to spend hours staring at a computer screen in the hopes that someone will post a supportive comment about the party we went to last Friday, or the fight we had Tuesday night with our girlfriend? Just three years ago, meeting someone on the Internet was worthy of being cast to the bottom rung of the social ladder. Now, thanks to MySpace, meeting people via the Internet is not only socially acceptable, but there is a certain level of coolness to having tons of friends on your MySpace page.

Don't like a friend? Delete them. Don't want someone's opinion? Ban their input. Don't like the way you look? Simply change your photo. You can be who you want, when you want, with whom you want. In fact, it's so perfect and so addictive that it's easy to spend all of our time there, pouring ourselves into our own little MySpace kingdoms.

## Addicted to MySpace

I'm not certain how I finally realized that I was worshipping at the MySpace altar. Perhaps it was the fact that I was dragging in late to work as a result of late-night blogging. Maybe I realized I was spending more time talking to my new 'Internet' friends than my real-life college buddies. Perhaps it was the fact that the letters had begun to fade from my keyboard from the incessant typing. Whatever the reason, I am thankful. No matter how fun it is, an addiction is an addiction, and it is not a healthy thing. I knew that I had to do something before I lost my soul completely to the void of cyberspace, and so I hatched one final desperate plan. I've decided to quit MySpace for two weeks, cold turkey.

I'm not proposing a ban on MySpace or anything like that. In fact, I'm not even deleting my own profile. I'm simply saying that things like MySpace are only healthy when done in moderation. Logging a hundred hours of Internet time on MySpace is nowhere near as fulfilling as spending real face-to-face time with a good friend.

I posted one final blog advising the MySpace world that I was taking a bit of a 'MySpace sabbatical' to regain some focus. This has not been easy, but I figure that the new perspective on life will be well worth the time spent away from my Mac iBook. In the past few days since leaving MySpace, I've gone for a walk, watched *Hotel Rwanda* (something I'd been swearing I'd do for months now) and started a great book. Last night, I even spent some time with my best friend, sitting on his front porch and talking about life, work, and faith. He has a new job, and I'm happy for him. He began to tell me all about the great day he'd had and for a moment, I thought, "This would make such a great blog," before suddenly catching myself. I was wrong. This makes for great life.

# Web Resources

**All Things Web 2.0**

www.allthingsweb2.com

An extensive list of Web 2.0 sites, including several Top 100 lists.

**Blog Herald**

www.blogherald.com

The longest-standing source of blog-related news, founded in 2003. In addition to daily news about the blogosphere it contains editorials, reviews, and tutorials.

**Blogger**

www.blogger.com

One of the major blog hosting services. It is owned and operated by Google and is free.

**Blogger's Choice Awards**

http://bloggerschoiceawards.com

Allows users to vote for the best blog of the year in many different categories.

**Bloglines**

www.blogline.com

A free online service for searching, subscribing, creating, and sharing news feeds, blogs, and rich Web content. It allows readers to search for, read, and share updates from their favorite news feed or blog, regardless of its authoring technology, at a single site. This content can also be accessed from handheld computers and mobile phones.

## Cyberjournalist
www.cyberjournalist.net

A news and resource site that focuses on how the Internet, convergence, and new technologies are changing the media. It offers tips, news, and commentary about online journalism, citizen's media, digital storytelling, converged news operations, and using the Internet as a reporting tool.

## Delicious
http://delicious.com

A popular social bookmarking site, where users can organize and share their favorite Web sites.

## Digg
http://digg.com

A site where users share their favorite Web sites, videos, and newscasts.

## Facebook
www.facebook.com

One of the major social networking sites, Facebook tends to be preferred by college students and adults.

## Flickr
www.flickr.com

A major photo sharing site.

## Google Reader
www.google.com/reader/view/#overview-page

One of the major RSS readers, Google Reader provides a place to read updates from blogs selected by the user.

## Learning 2.1: Explore . . . Discover . . . Play
http://explorediscoverplay.blogspot.com

A blog devoted to discovering and discussing new and interesting Web 2.0 tools and sites.

## LibraryThing
www.librarything.com

A site that allows users to catalog their personal book collection and share reviews and recommendations.

## LinkedIn
www.linkedin.com

One of the major social networking sites, LinkedIn focuses on business and professional networking.

## LiveJournal
www.livejournal.com

One of the major blog hosting services.

## MySpace
www.myspace.com

One of the major social networking sites, MySpace tends to be preferred by teens.

## Ning
www.ning.com

A site that hosts user-created social networks.

## Reddit
www.reddit.com

A site where users share what is new and popular online.

## Technorati
www.technorati.com

The Internet's primary blog search engine. As of 2007 it is tracking 109.1 million blogs and over 250 million pieces of tagged social media. Its site has daily lists of the most popular blogs and offers the ability to search all blogs by topic or keyword. Individuals can indicate their favorite blogs and can easily see what other blogs have linked to their own.

### Twitter
http://twitter.com

A microblogging site where people answer the question "what are you doing?" in 140 characters or less. Many people use a mobile device to Twitter.

### WordPress
http://wordpress.com

One of the major blog hosting services.

### YouTube
www.youtube.com

One of the major video sharing sites.

# For Further Research

## Books

Tyrone L. Adams and Stephen A. Smith, *Electronic Tribes: The Virtual Worlds of Geeks, Gamers, Shamans, and Scammers*. Austin: University of Texas Press, 2008.

Terry Burrows, *Blogs, Wikis, MySpace, and More: Everything You Want to Know About Using Web 2.0 but Are Afraid to Ask*. Chicago: Chicago Review Press, 2007.

Anastasia Goodstein, *Totally Wired: What Teens and Tweens Are Really Doing Online*. New York: St. Martin's Griffin, 2007.

Jason Illian, *My Space, My Kids*. Eugene, OR: Harvest House, 2007.

Bradley L. Jones, *Web 2.0 Heroes: Interviews with 20 Web 2.0 Influencers*. Indianapolis: Wiley, 2008.

Andrew Keen, *The Cult of the Amateur: How Blogs, MySpace, YouTube, and the Rest of Today's User-Generated Media Are Destroying Our Economy, Our Culture, and Our Values*. New York: Currency Doubleday, 2007.

John Palfrey and Urs Gasser, *Born Digital: Understanding the First Generation of Digital Natives*. New York: Basic Books, 2008.

Jill Walker Rettberg, *Blogging*. Cambridge, UK: Polity Press, 2008.

## Periodicals

Steven M. Cohen, "I Twittered, Then I 'Tumbld' . . . ," *Information Today*, May 1, 2007.

N'Gai Croal, "The Peril of Digital Fidgeting," *Newsweek*, July 21, 2008.

Michael Duffy, "A Dad's Encounter with the Vortex of Facebook," *Time (Canadian edition)*, March 27, 2006.

Justin Fox, "You're Among Friends," *Time*, July 16, 2007.

Mariel Garza, "Excuse Me, I'm Tied Up Blogging," *Los Angeles Daily News*, June 10, 2007.

Emily Gould, "Exposed," *New York Times Magazine*, May 25, 2008.

David Grimes, "A Web Site About Nothing," *Sarasota (FL) Herald-Tribune*, November 18, 2007.

Becky Hogge, "Beware of Online Friendship," *New Statesman*, July 9, 2007.

Becky Hogge, "Welcome to Meatspace: You Might Think I Spend All My time in the Virtual World, but Really I Don't," *New Statesman*, April 30, 2007.

Julia James, "Leave Facbeook—If You Can," *University Wire*, March 2, 2006.

John Kelly, "How They Found Me: The Word Searches That Bring People to My Blog Reflect a World of Fetish, Pathology, and Itchiness," *Guardian (Manchester, UK)*, April 21, 2008.

Tricia King, "Facebook Has Its Charms, but It's Not Doing Much for my Senioritis," *Norfolk Virginian Pilot*, January 18, 2008.

Robert MacMillan, "A Blog by Any Other Name," *Washington Post*, August 25, 2005.

Lon Matejczyk, "Taking the Plunge into Social Networking with Facebook," *Colorado Springs Business Journal*, September 26, 2008.

Tim O'Reilly, "What Is Web 2.0?" www.oreillynet.com, September 30, 2005.

Kurt Soller, "Why I Love It . . ." *Newsweek*, August 27, 2007.

Joel Stein, "You Are Not My Friend," *Time*, October 15, 2007.

Agnieszka Tennant, "A Fishy Facebook Friend," *Christianity Today*, October 2007.

Jackie Lee Thomas, "When 'Goodbye' Is a Click Away," *Newsweek*, December 3, 2007.

Janice Turner, "My Facebook Agony: What If I Get Un-friended?" *Times* (London), September 1, 2007.

Craig Wilson, "Suddenly, You've Got a Friend—Tons of Them," *USA Today*, February 6, 2008.

# Index